D1231162

UNLIKELY ASSASSINS

The shocking true story of a
couple savagely murdered by
their own teenage daughter

M.E. COOPER

J. FLORES PUBLICATIONS
P.O. Box 830131
Miami, FL 33283-0131

UNLIKELY ASSASSINS by M.E. Cooper

Copyright © 1992 by M.E. Cooper

Published by:
J. Flores Publications
P.O. Box 830131
Miami, FL 33283-0131

Direct inquires and/or order to the above address.

ISBN 0-918751-25-X

Library of Congress Catalog Card Number: 91-77249

Printed in the United States of America

About the Author

M.E. Cooper is a native Oklahoman. She lives in Stillwater, Oklahoma with her husband. She enjoys reading, riding motorcycles and traveling with her husband, who is an antique bicycle collector.

to the Stillwater Writers
who gave me so much encouragement

Chapter One

A scream split the early morning air in the prosperous, well-kept neighborhood, followed by the sound of running footsteps to the neighboring house. Pounding on the door, the slight, young woman in blue jeans cried, "My parents have been murdered. Call the police!" Her short reddish hair was in disarray, and her normally pale face with its scattering of ·freckles, was flushed from exertion. The houses were separated by both distance and a wooden fence. Each residence was built on a spacious lot. "Open the door! Call the police!" She was shouting now, hammering at the door with her fist.

Larry Wynn, still foggy from sleep at six twenty a.m. could scarcely credit what he was hearing. His neighbor's daughter, Francine Stepp, was alternately screaming and crying that her parents were dead. He and his wife knew the Stepp family well. Their own rebellious daughter was a friend of Francine's. With a sense of disbelief he called the police.

Police Dispatcher Debbie Rice notified relief Sergeant John Jerkin.

"Responding Code three!" With lights flashing and siren going Jerkin raced from the Kay-Bobs restaurant parking lot in the 700 block of North Main Street. He had just finished breakfast and was the closest officer to 4823 Rogers Drive, on the north edge of Stillwater, Oklahoma.

He noticed that the skies were clear and there was enough daylight so he could drive without headlights. Jerkin pulled up in front of the address. He was met by the neighbor who was shirtless and barefoot, wearing blue jeans.

"Their daughter's at our house. She says they're both dead."

"Have you been inside?"

"No. I think they're upstairs."

Jerkin knew that correct police procedure would be to wait for backup. On the other hand, victims could be bleeding to death inside. He decided in an instant that it was more important to render assistance. He walked back to his patrol car. "Unit nine to Headquarters. I'm ten-ninety-seven," meaning, arrived at location. "I'm entering residence now." The front glass storm door was closed, but the front door was standing slightly open. Heart pounding, Jerkin advanced up the stairway and turned left to a bedroom. It was dim inside the house. Aware that he might be jumped if the perpetrator were hiding somewhere, he advanced with gun drawn and his flashlight in his other hand.

He saw no bodies in any of the upstairs bedrooms or the connecting bathroom. In the still, quiet morning he could hear an electronic beeping sound. It sounded like a telephone left off the hook or possibly a clock radio. He went back downstairs toward the master bedroom. In the hallway he observed a spent .22 long rifle caliber shell casing on the floor. He did not touch it, but peered through the partially open doorway.

Mark Stepp was lying face up on the blood-drenched bed. His face was very pale and sunken. There was no sound of breathing or movement of his chest. His wife, Delores Stepp lay on her side on the blood-soaked carpet. Her back was toward the officer. The wooden handle of a kitchen knife protruded from her body. Jerkin did not touch the bodies. The blood was slightly congealed and it was obvious they were beyond help.

Jerkin observed the slightly open patio door that led to a concrete patio surrounded by a wooden privacy fence. The patio was empty.

The ambulance from Stillwater Fire Department No. 3 station arrived in front of the residence. Jerkin was grateful for some company.

"I'd like you to verify that the victims are deceased."

The next call Debbie received at Police Headquarters was a slightly breathless one from the sergeant. "We have two homicides. I have secured the area. Suggest you notify Division Commander."

Corporal Jim Harrison, veteran officer on the force was the next to arrive. He was immediately told, "Check out the victim's daughter at 105 Audene, the house next door on the corner. She was the one who found them."

Two more policemen arrived and Jerkin told them to go into the back yard of the neighboring house to observe any entry or exit. And to stay out of the back yard of the Stepps' residence due to the possibility of more .22 caliber shell casings or other evidence that might be disturbed. With the arrival of another Officer, named Pangborn, Jerkin strung the yellow barrier tape marked "Police Line - Do Not Cross."

On the evening of the last day of his life, Mark Stepp mowed his lawn with a power mower. He did not quite finish mowing and left it where he stopped, leaving one strip of long grass in the otherwise immaculately kept yard. On an ordinary workday he would have driven south to Stillwater on Highway 177 from his job at the Sooner Generating Plant, run by Oklahoma Gas & Electric. The road passes rolling hills dotted with fat, white-faced Herefords. Farm ponds dot the landscape, as does an occasional scenic windmill. Past Black Bear Creek, there is a herd of dairy Holstein cattle and some sleek quarter-horses grazing in the pastures.

On the last evening of his life the beauty of the southwest landscape was never more apparent as he drove on the road above the Cimarron Turnpike that runs through Oklahoma from east to west. He drove past the railroad tracks, now seldom used, to the twelve mile corner with its Jiffy Stop gas station and grocery. Then approaching Stillwater, he would have driven by Lakeside Memorial Golf Course with its immaculately kept greens and sand traps. The highway follows Perkins Road until the turn-off to Rogers Addition. A sign bears the information "Thirty-one Acres, Tennis and Swimming Pool."

Mark Stepp was a good-looking man, with a thick head of wavy hair, mustache, and a compact, muscular body. He had just returned from Memorial Day weekend holiday in Kansas and planned to go to work the next morning.

Turning into his driveway, he surely felt pride at his circumstances. The comfortable four bedroom, two and a half bath home faced the north and a strip of green belt, giving the illusion of country living, with the advantage of near neighbors. The two car garage was joined by a wooden privacy fence. He watered the lawn that day, keeping it as green as the nearby golf course.

Delores Stepp was "Dee" to her friends and co-workers. She had a much shorter drive than her husband's eighteen miles commute to work. On a normal working day, Dee left the accounting office on the third floor of Whitehurst Hall on the campus of Oklahoma State University. Behind her, the library chimes rang out the hour each evening at five. She would have walked toward the parking lot, while students walked past her to the fountain splashing in front of the red brick library building with its white bell tower reminiscent of Independence Hall.

Driving down Monroe street, she would have turned on University Avenue, past the formal gardens and picturesque Theta pond. She might have glanced over at the couples sitting on the benches under the weeping willow trees or watched the ducks frolicking in the water.

As Mark and Dee ate their last meal together, they might have talked of their previous home in Fond Du Lac, Wisconsin, and complained of the Oklahoma summers. Mark had met Dee while he served in the United States Navy. He had learned electronic technology in the service and was well paid by Oklahoma Gas and Electric.

Dee was a handsome woman, full-figured and muscular. She worked in the accounting department at Oklahoma State University. They had every right to feel that they had it made. Their one child and only daughter dropped out of her freshman year in college, but she was working at the university and they expected she would enroll for the fall semester. Dee found satisfaction in managing a softball team, while Mark enjoyed belonging to the Moose Lodge. They had just returned from a short trip to a nudist camp in Hutchinson, Kansas.

Had the person who overheard the plotting of their murders contacted them, would they have believed it possible that anyone would want them dead? It seemed so improbable that the plotters could be serious, that the witness dismissed it from his mind.

So their last evening alive was spent in ordinary ways, with not the slightest hint that they might not arise the next morning.

Sometime between nine thirty p.m. and eleven thirty p.m. Mark and Dee Stepp were startled out of their sleep by the sound of their bedroom door being violently kicked open. Two shadowy figures in the darkened room loomed over them. Gunshots rang out. Four bullets hit the wall over the bed, but one bullet entered Mark Stepps neck, effectively paralyzing him. He must have seen his killer and the knife descending to his chest, but he was unable to defend himself. He died where he lay, from eight stab wounds that severed the aorta of his heart.

Then it was Delores' time of agony. She managed to get off the bed, trying to escape her killer. She reached frantically for the bedside phone, but it was wrenched from her hand. The knife blade was plunged into her chest again and again. A strong and athletic person, she was still unable to escape her killer. She turned away from the terrifying knife, trapped between the bed, the wall and the dresser. There was no escaping the death blows. Nineteen times the blade penetrated her body. Finally the knife was thrust into her back and left embedded there.

No alarm was raised, no one in the neighborhood was aware that violent and bloody death had taken the lives of the forty-year-old couple that lived in one of the nicest areas of the town, of one of the safest cities in the US.

Stillwater is located in the north central part of Oklahoma. The Chamber of Commerce is housed in a one-story brick building on the Main street. Their members are justifiably proud of the community of forty-two thousand residents. Home of the second largest university in the state, Stillwater boasts of a crime rate one half the national average. A community where there are over twice as many churches as beer taverns and bars. A good place to raise children. A city that prides itself on its friendliness. Stillwater has a small town atmosphere with the recreational and cultural advantages usually found only in large communities. The murders of Mark and Dee Stepp shocked and stunned the community.

It was six forty-five a.m. when Detective Sergeant Billy Bartram received the call from headquarters. He was in Oklahoma City attending a Criminal Investigation School, when he was told of the double murder and instructed to get back to Stillwater as quickly as possible.

Within minutes, not taking time for breakfast, Bartram was on Interstate 35, heading north for Stillwater. About the same time, calls were going out to Oklahoma State Bureau of Investigation, the Federal Bureau of Investigation and State Coroner's office. The ponderous machinery of law enforcement and investigation was getting under way.

When Bartram pulled into the drive at the Stepp home, he saw that the yellow tape denoting a crime scene was in place. Lieutenant Ron Thrasher, division commander of the criminal investigation department was videotaping the interior of the house. Bartram spoke to Corporal Dennis McGrath, a long time friend and associate. They had worked together on past crimes. McGrath's usually cheerful grin was nowhere evident this morning. Suicides and accidental deaths were not that unusual, but the gruesome reality inside the home had shaken most of the men.

Lieutenant Thrasher, head of the criminal investigation department spoke to the men. His heavy dark eyebrows drawn together in a frown of concentration. "Bartram, I'm assigning you and McGrath as primary case investigators. Shearer and Treadwell, you've got the responsibility for processing the crime scene."

They put on the plastic gloves and bootees over their shoes to prevent contamination of the crime scene and entered the building to listen to the lieutenant's further instructions.

Thrasher is a dark complexioned man, wiry and muscular, about five feet seven inches tall. He spoke to the men assembled "Now, I don't want you to get in a hurry here and overlook any evidence. Those people in there aren't going to mind if it takes you all day. I want you to take your time and do things step by step."

"Stepp by Stepp." The men echoed the words and there were a few snickers. During the long, tense day, when men would have to go outside for a breath of fresh air, as the horror of the scene became too much for them, someone would mutter under his breath, "Just take it Stepp by Stepp." And it brought a little gallows humor to an otherwise grim job.

Since he was primary case investigator, Bartram requested Officer Shaw and Treadwell examine the vehicles parked outside the house. He felt the vehicles might contain evidence which should not be destroyed. The men began by searching the black Chevrolet Camaro that Francine normally drove, as well as the Trans Am that Delores took pride in, and the old pickup that Mark drove to work. They continued until all the vehicles had been searched.

Outside the house Corporal Harrison was observing the Stepps' daughter, Francine. She stood outside the house, nonchalantly watching the comings and goings of the police department. He noted that she was slim and small, probably weighing not much over one hundred pounds. She was wearing a short sleeved blouse and blue jeans. Far from hysterical, she seemed unnaturally calm. He and McGrath commented to each other on the strangeness of her behavior.

The ambulance sat out front with its lights still flashing. Harrison approached the ambulance driver, who was a paramedic on the Stillwater Fire department.

"Would you do me a favor?"

"Sure thing. What would you like?"

"Take her blood pressure." Harrison nodded toward Francine. "She's too calm. She's gotta be feeling something, walking into a blood bath like that. I don't want her collapsing on us or something."

"Okay." A short while later, the ambulance driver walked over to Harrison.

"Guess what? Her blood pressure's normal."

"You've got to be kidding!"

"No! I took it twice to be sure."

In the hallway outside the master bedroom, a .22 casing lay on the floor. Upstairs, Bartram observed the storage room containing weightlifting and exercise equipment, ironing board, and other bulky items. A bathroom with twin sinks and garden tub appeared untouched. Francine's room had football pennants by the doorway, featuring the Denver Broncos and the Philadelphia Eagles. A calendar with the singing group Alabama on it hung on the wall. Two rows of stuffed animals lined the opposite wall and more stuffed animals were visible in the open closet. A study desk under a hanging lamp and single bed made up the room of an average teenager.

Downstairs, in the Stepps' bedroom, the policemen were continuing their exhaustive investigation. The bloody phone had the cord ripped out of the phone itself. The black-tiled bathroom, with its garden tub and hanging lamp yielded no clues. The police observed the books in the bookcase.

Most of the volumes were sex manuals and books about sex. The numerous magazines scattered about were nudist magazines. There were commercial X-rated videotapes and three that were labeled by hand, as well as a video camera and tripod. On the nightstand by the bed was a half-filled glass of wine, and an empty wine bottle was in the wastebasket. Plainly visible through the closet doors was Mark Stepp's coin collection.

There was no evidence of robbery. The Federal Bureau of Investigation responded to the department's request for help with a statistical composite of the killers. Stillwater police investigators were told that in all probability the perpetrators had been two white males, ages nineteen to twenty-five, from urban backgrounds, drug addicts, who had possibly killed animals, prior to these murders, and who might be driving a pickup truck.

The local radio station, KSPI, broadcast an appeal for anyone seeing a pickup truck in the area the night of the murders, or anyone seeing anything unusual to please contact the police department.

Lieutenant Thrasher contacted Francine at the residence immediately east of her parent's home, the Larry Wynn's residence. She asked him to notify her relatives and gave him the phone numbers. The lieutenant sent Teletypes to the police authorities of the respective cities to deliver death notifications. A minister from the Methodist church had already been summoned by an officer, and he lingered awhile, trying to provide spiritual support to the sole survivor of the Mark Stepp family.

Cindy Wynn arrived then, asking, "What are all the police cars doing here?"

Lieutenant Thrasher asked Cindy Wynn to step into another room, where he proceeded to interview Francine's best friend. He studied the girl sitting in front of him. Cindy had a round face, big blue eyes, straight short nose and cherubic smile. Her hair was bleached blonde, showing a little dark at the roots.

In response to Thrasher's question concerning her whereabouts the previous night, Cindy replied that she was home. She referred to Randy Jackson's apartment as "home", despite the fact they were sitting in her parents' house, plus another young woman had arrived at the crime scene who said she was Cindy's roommate at an entirely different address.

"I got off work at Pizza Hut," Cindy told the lieutenant, "The one on North Boomer Road and I went to 802 Highpoint, Apartment Twenty one. Then Frankie came over."

"You mean Francine?"

"Yeah, we all call her Frankie. She came over and we sat and talked, then she left to go baby-sitting. Said she'd be back about twelve thirty. Then my boyfriend Randall

Jackson came home. Then Frankie came back. Randy wanted to go over to a friend's house to watch the Lakers game, and I asked Frankie to take him, but she said no, because he's black and her parents might see him in the car with her and get mad about it."

"Then what happened?"

"Randy left, walking, and Frankie and me left to go driving around. We stopped at Boomer Lake Park and visited with some friends. Then we went to Frankie's house, but I did not see her parents."

"Go on."

"We sat and talked awhile. Then we walked over to Jack Griffith's gas station to get a couple of Cokes. Then we went to bed and set the alarm for six thirty this morning."

"What were the sleeping arrangements?"

"I slept with Randy and Frankie slept on the couch. She woke up before us because I remember her standing at the foot of the bed and then telling us she'd be back about nine o'clock." Cindy paused for a moment, then added, "Oh yes, I remember when we were at Frankie's house, Frankie told me, 'Make sure that the door is locked, I get in trouble if the door is left unlocked.'"

Lieutenant Thrasher told her gently, "Francine's parents are dead. They were murdered last night."

Cindy became very emotional. "Oh my God! They were just starting to work things out! Her parents and her get along so good except over my boyfriend."

Lieutenant Thrasher concluded his interview with Cindy and returned to the crime scene.

Downtown Stillwater was a buzz with rumors and speculation. At the banks, in the post office, on the downtown streets, people would stop each other and relay the latest rumor. "I heard it on good authority that it was a group of Satan worshippers." "I heard their bodies were mutilated." People were aghast at the whispered reports. Each retelling seemed to add to the lurid misinformation that was circulating.

Meanwhile, the police were continuing their examination and search for clues to the killer or killers.

Officer R. Dickerson was following orders and conducting a house-to-house canvas of the neighborhood. The neighbors to the west of the Stepps told him, "We saw them outside doing yard work yesterday evening, until about nine o'clock or possibly even ten o'clock." They had heard nothing during the night.

Another neighbor confided that she thought the Stepps daughter seemed pretty wild, and had a boyfriend who drove an off-white truck with a loud exhaust, and she thought that he had been at the residence the previous evening.

Dickerson continued questioning neighbors. Of the nine households nearest the murdered couple, none of the residents had seen or heard anything unusual.

As the officers worked the crime scene, collecting hair samples and examining the vehicles for evidence, they conjectured about the crime.

"We know both Mark and Dee were strong, active people, so that, even if surprised out of a sound sleep, it seems logical they could have fought off a lone attacker."

"So you think there were more than one."

"It seems that way to me."

Six spent .22 caliber casings were located and collected, after being photographed and measured. The first spent casing was the obvious one in the hallway. The others were found just inside the master bedroom door, three in front of the dresser and one behind the dresser.

Bartram and McGrath both noticed that Francine Stepp had called her boyfriend while the police examination of the crime scene was going on. They were waiting in the front yard of the Stepp residence. He had his arm around her and they were cuddling up to each other.

"They act like they're at the lake!"

"She sure doesn't behave like you would expect someone who's just found her parents murdered."

"She may not have liked her parents much, but young girls don't commit homicides like this one!" They dismissed the couple as suspects from their minds and continued searching for evidence in the house.

Upstairs, the air-conditioning was working perfectly, but the downstairs was not receiving the benefit of the cool air. It was ninety five degrees inside the bedroom. Several of the men complained about the bloody smell. They would pale and have to leave the room to get fresh air. "I don't notice it, myself," Bartram commented.

"It's because your nose's been broken twice," McGrath responded.

"No, that isn't it." One of the other men responded, "It's because he smells so much horse shit, he can't smell anything any more."

All the men enjoyed kidding Bartram about his hobby.

"Now, I'm telling you, horses are the most beautiful, *honest* creatures on the earth."

"Yeah, and cleaning out stables is just a fun way to spend your spare time!"

Bartram instructed an officer to check all the pawnshops in the area for any .22 caliber guns they had sold in the past few months. Receiving the Dickerson's news that a neighbor thought the boyfriend's pickup had been at the house on the evening of the murder, McGrath took a closer view of Francine's boyfriend.

"What's your name, son?"

"Fred Rank," the blond haired youth replied.

"Are you a student or are you employed somewhere?"

"I work full time at Vassar Manufacturing in Perkins."

"Do you own a gun?"

"Just a .22 rifle."

"Hmm. Let me talk to my partner for a minute." They decided to send Officer Jim O'Daniel to accompany Fred to retrieve the rifle. Fred was informed of his rights, fingerprinted and the officer followed him the ten miles to the small town of 1500 population just south of Stillwater.

"That gun hasn't been fired in years!" Fred's family insisted when they saw Fred giving the officer the rifle and receiving a receipt for it. O'Daniel felt the members were friendly so he asked casually, "Fred ever been in trouble with the law?"

"Nothing but a DUI, and that can happen to anybody that drinks more than two beers on a Saturday night." O'Daniel nodded. "As far as you know, Fred got along with Francine's parents all right?"

"Never been any hard feelings that I know of." They all agreed.

Officers in the field were combing the reports of traffic violations occurring during the previous night, the night of the murder. A recently released felon and known troublemaker had been stopped on Perkins Road not far from the crime. An officer had observed some youths drinking beer in the vicinity of the Rogers Addition swimming pool. They were nervous at being questioned, and the policeman discovered that they had been climbing over the fence instead of using the key provided residents. An officer reported seeing a Caucasian female run from the southeast corner of Audene and Rogers Drive to the southwest corner of the street intersection between midnight and one a.m. He was about two hundred yards away and southbound.

At the crime scene, the lieutenant came in then and asked, "Are we about finished here?"

By this time, Nicki Graham and Ray Blakeney from the medical examiner's office were waiting to remove the bodies to Oklahoma City for autopsy. The hands of the victims were covered with paper bags, to prevent loss of evidence that might be lodged under their fingernails. They were wrapped in new white sheets furnished by the Stillwater Police Department and placed in black zippered body bags for their removal from the house. Dee Stepp's body had to be transported face down to keep the knife intact.

Waiting television cameras caught the picture, which was shown on the ten o'clock news that night. Primary case investigator Bartram was chagrinned to see his picture on the front page of the *News Press* accompanying the bodies out of the house. He had not changed clothes from early morning when he had dashed from the hotel in Oklahoma City. He was wearing a T-shirt with two drunken cats on it and one of them was saying, Are We Having Fun Yet?

The detectives responsible for processing the crime scene had a multitude of duties. Collecting fibers, human hair, and any other evidence relevant to the crime. They removed the blood-smeared doorknob to the master bedroom as well as the bloody telephone. Treadwell used a power saw to cut the sheet rock out around the bullet holes. He used a screwdriver and chipped into two separate support 2x4s and located two bullets. There were markings in the brick wall that indicated the other two bullets had gone through the sheet rock, missed the 2x4s and struck the wall. Once the four bullets hit the wall, they had traveled in an unknown direction. Five bullets were accounted for. One bullet was lodged in Mark Stepp's neck and the other one was never found. A box of .22 caliber long rifle rounds were discovered in the master bedroom, but no weapon.

Each doorway was examined for pry marks indicating forcible entry. The garage was checked as well as the front door, the patio door and all the windows. The officers could not find any evidence that the intruders had pried their way in.

In the kitchen, Treadwell found a handwritten poem on a yellow note pad that stated, "Get on a ship, go afar," and concluded with the last line, "Get a knife."

In the living room couch, tucked down between the pillows, was a note that read: "Francine is going to spend the night with Cindy." Obviously, the writer anticipated objections from the parents, because the note contained several excuses. Each excuse was crossed off, as the writer had tried to improve on the explanation.

Francine was asked to come to the police station to answer questions.

The Stillwater Police Department is located in one part of the municipal building. Behind the glass doors of the foyer, with its information window, another glass door leads to the green-tiled hallway and stairs to the detectives offices on the second floor.

In the morning, the next day after the murder, Francine Stepp appeared with Cindy Wynn, her girlfriend and alibi for the night of the murder. Francine was invited to answer questions alone. Cindy waited outside the room. Francine was wearing blue jeans, and a sleeveless blouse. Dennis McGrath observed the pallor of her face, seeing the freckles standing out against the whiteness of her skin. Her face was slender, her nose prominent, a little flattened at the end. She was not wearing glasses and her green eyes were a little glassy looking, due to contact lenses. Francine had full lips, with rather prominent teeth, straight and white. Long earrings dangled from her ears, contrasting with the almost masculine cut of her flaming red hair. He thought that she would be an attractive young woman if she smiled.

McGrath smoothed his mustache with his hand and smiled at Francine. He is a slender young man, affable and friendly. Bartram stood to one side of the desk, his arms crossed, a solemn expression on his usually cheerful face. Aware that she must be suffering from the trauma of seeing her parents dead, McGrath was careful and gentle as he spoke.

"Now just tell me what happened day before yesterday evening."

"Well, I got off work about nine o'clock and went straight home. Then I got a call from my boyfriend. I ate supper and then I went to Cindy's apartment on High Point. We stayed there until about eleven thirty."

"Then what did you do?"

"We went to my house and talked with my parents about a softball tournament and I asked if I could spend the night with Cindy. My mother said it was okay as long as I was back early in the morning. We went back to Cindy's apartment and stayed there until six o'clock this morning."

They went over this information several times. Francine added, "We drove around Boomer Lake some and talked with some of Cindy's friends at the lake. We went back to my house to get a change of clothes, and then we went to Cindy's apartment for the rest of the night."

"Now, I have to ask you this, Francine. When we examined the bedroom where your parents were killed, we found pictures of your parents in the nude, along with nudist magazines. Were you ever sexually abused by your parents?"

"No! I was not."

"We found pictures of you with your parents, and all of you were nude," Bartram showed her one taken with her mother as they were sliding down a slide.

"I was only about four years old at the time! I never took off my clothes except when family was around."

The detectives told Francine she was free to go. Then it was time to interview Cindy Wynn. The men knew their lieutenant had already talked with Cindy, but they wanted to hear her version of the night's events.

Cindy Wynn reminded the detective of Molly Ringwald, the teenage actress. With full cheeks and a "baby face" Cindy had a vivacious manner that made it easy to talk with her. Francine had been very quiet and sullen, appearing to have a chip on her shoulder. Cindy chatted easily about the night of the murder.

Detective Bartram urged her to relax and be calm. "Now, I want you to tell me about your activities on the evening before the murders. Just start at the beginning and tell me things as you remember them."

"Francine came over to my apartment at 802 High Point. At about nine thirty p.m., Francine and I and my boyfriend went downstairs. My boyfriend went off by himself and we drove around for awhile."

"Yes, go on."

"Francine asked if she could spend the night. We drove to her parents' house, but we didn't see them, so we left again. About midnight, my boyfriend came back. I'd forgotten my cigarettes and some change on the counter at Francine's house, so we went back to get them."

"Now, this is important. Did you both go into the house?"

"Yes, we did. But we didn't see her parents."

"Then what did you do?"

"We went back to my apartment and sat and talked. About three o'clock we went to Jack Griffith's gas station and got some Cokes, and then we went back to 802 High Point and set the alarm for 6:30 and went to sleep."

"Were you at any time alone, during the course of the evening?"

"No, I was with Francine all evening."

"Could she have slipped out of your apartment without you knowing it?"

"No. We were together all evening."

Cindy Wynn was informed that she was free to go. Detective Bartram did not reveal to Cindy that her testimony conflicted with Francine's, but he looked at her so steadily that she was nervous. Later, she would tell friends that Sergeant Bartram scared her.

The detectives were now busy assessing the information that was beginning to pour in from concerned citizens. There were sightings of pickup trucks and strange men.

"Maybe we'll get lucky and the perps who did this will get stopped for running a red light."

"Yeah, and maybe I'll win the Missouri lottery, too."

"It happens more often than you think. If the FBI is right, the killers were high and they may be stopped for speeding in another state."

"Let's just hope it's not a rookie cop who walks up to them and gets his head blown off."

"Amen to that."

Neighbors revealed to the investigators that Francine and her parents had argued bitterly only a few days previous to the murder. The police were told that Cindy Wynn's stepmother, Mitzi Wynn, had spoken to Dee Stepp shortly before the murders. They were told that Mitzi confided to Dee that they had given up attempting to control their rebellious daughter. She felt that Cindy was determined to anger and humiliate them. Her latest tactic was to date interracially.

"Francine seems like a good girl." Mitzi had warned her next-door neighbor, "If you want to keep her out of trouble, keep her away from Cindy."

From interviews, the investigators learned that Dee Stepp was an aggressive and dominating personality. She could be abrasive at times. According to Dee's acquaintances, she had ordered her daughter to discontinue her friendship with Cindy Wynn. This struck the officers as strange, in light of Francine's testimony that her mother had not objected to her spending the night with Cindy. Who was telling the truth here?

McGrath and Bartram discussed possibilities. "Maybe we should take a look at the boyfriends. If one or both of them were mad enough to kill, they might have committed murder. Francine was an only child, and she would inherit the house and the cars."

"That doesn't seem like much motive for murder."

"People have been killed for a lot less."

On the theory that the victims might have known their murderers, the detectives went back out to the crime scene and watched the videotapes that the Stepps had made.

"It seems uncanny," Bartram noted to his friend. "One morning we are examining their bodies and this evening we're watching them frolicking happily in their home video."

They discovered that the Stepps vacation weekend had been spent at a nudist camp. There was a picture of another couple in the nude with Mark and Dee Stepp, and they resolved to try to find the identity of the couple.

"What do you think? One of them could have been cheating and a jilted lover was enraged enough to do this?"

"Perhaps. Since nothing was taken, that tends to discount the crazed dope addict looking for something to pawn or sell for another fix, as far as I'm concerned. So what does that leave?"

"Just the whole country full of serial killer maniacs, that's all."

"That's real encouraging."

It was after midnight before the tired detectives finally parted company to go home.

Chapter Two

Reporting for work, Sergeant Billy Bartram wanted to know: "What's on the agenda for today?"

Even before Lieutenant Thrasher could commence his instructions, the phone rang. Francine Stepp was on the telephone, "There is one thing missing from my house. A blue key ring with keys on it."

"Can you describe it?"

"It's just a blue plastic key ring with five keys on it."

"Okay, we'll put out a notice on that."

Relaying the information to the detectives, the Lieutenant sounded skeptical. Bartram uttered what they were all thinking: "That's really strange. In a house with all kinds of valuables to sell, a killer takes a key ring."

The daily Stillwater newspaper, the *News Press*, dutifully ran an article describing the blue key ring and asking anyone finding it to immediately contact the police department.

Later in the day, Cindy Wynn called the police department. She sounded frantic with fear. "Someone called me this morning and told me I was next. And just now, coming out into the Wal-Mart parking lot, I was nearly run over. Someone is trying to kill me!"

The officer tried to calm the girl and get more information. "Did you get a license tag number, even a partial number?"

"No! I was too shaken up. I could have been killed!"

"Could you describe the vehicle to me?"

"No! It was dark colored, but that's about all I can tell you."

"Well then, about this voice on the telephone, was it a man's voice or a woman's voice?"

"I don't know!" Cindy nearly howled. She was sobbing and crying. "Why are you asking me stupid questions?"

She was incoherent and the officer tried to calm her.

"Don't you realize my life's in danger? I might have been killed!"

The officer soothed the sobbing teenager and promised they would look into the matter. He drove out to Wal-Mart, but none of the clerks recalled hearing any squealing tires or any reports of a near accident. He found no one to corroborate her story.

Later, he reported to the investigators about the incident, "I don't know what to think. She can't remember what the car looked like or what the person on the telephone sounded like, so I don't know if it really happened or if she is just a hysterical young girl."

"Well, having a bloody double murder take place next door to her parents' house would be enough to make a lot of teenagers hysterical." McGrath sounded sympathetic.

It takes eight to ten weeks for an autopsy report to be completed and communicated from Oklahoma City, where it is performed, back to the District Attorney's office. The medical examiner does not work for the police department; she works for the District Attorney. Within twenty four hours, usually, the preliminary findings are called back to the headquarters, to aid with their investigation.

As the lieutenant reported the early results of the autopsies to the detectives investigating the murders, the mood of the men was somber. They were learning some of the things that had puzzled them.

"There was an alcohol content of .09 in his blood. That might explain his slow reaction time."

"Being awakened by someone intending to kill you would stun most people enough to slow their reactions."

"The .22 caliber bullet that penetrated his neck paralyzed him. That's why there were no signs that Mark Stepp tried to fight off his attacker."

"Poor soul! Dying from stab wounds and unable to defend himself!"

"Maybe the paralysis kept him from feeling the stab wounds."

"Well, it's a cinch his wife felt them!"

"Eighteen stab wounds! Some of them so deep they carried silicone from her breast implants into the lung itself!"

"She tried to fend off her killer. Did you hear the Lieutenant describe the deep stab wound on her right wrist?"

"Yes, it must have been when she threw up her hand to protect herself."

As the men discussed the findings from the medical officer's report, Bartram noted that the report was made by Dr. Chai S. Choi. "Have you ever met her?"

"Just briefly."

"I've always wanted to ask her if she watched *Quincy* on TV."

"Oh, you mean that old series about a police coroner?"

"Yeah."

"I'll bet that bears about as much resemblance to real life as the cop shows on TV do to our lives."

They all agreed with that.

"Do you think we'll find the killers who did this?"

"Well, we've got some fingerprints as soon as the Oklahoma Bureau matches them but if our perpetrators are drug addicts from good homes that have never been in trouble before it's going to make it almost impossible."

"Do you really think it was random serial killings? Two hop-heads that wanted to get a thrill by killing two people?"

"That's the hardest kind of case to solve, so I sure as hell hope not."

"If the Stepps' home had been on a highway, I would give more credence to the random killing theory, but it's about the farthest home from the entrance to Rogers Addition. You have to drive all over winding roads to get there, so that doesn't fit."

"Nothing fits the profile. I think we need to check out the boyfriends."

There followed routine police work, contacting the boyfriend of Francine Stepp, interviewing his parents, his fellow workers, following up and checking out his alibi for the time of the murders. He freely admitted telephoning Francine the evening of the murders. He gave his consent for the police to obtain the telephone records.

"So, what do we do now?"

"Unless I'm way off the mark, I think he'll check out clean. I think it's time we interviewed Cindy Wynn's live-in love."

"According to their accounts of that night he wasn't with them, but he was in the apartment from three a.m. until six a.m."

"Their stories don't match up. You'd think if they were all that close friends, and even a little bit smart, they would get their stories straight."

"Francine says she talked with her parents about softball and asked permission to spend the night, while Cindy says they didn't even see her parents. So which one is telling the truth?"

"I don't know, but let's go see what Cindy's boyfriend has to tell us."

They found his apartment, in one of several identical brick and redwood apartment buildings. They knocked on the door and the young black man invited them in.

Bartram and McGrath approached the subject casually. "Hey, Randall, I haven't seen you since you won the State Championship wrestling match at your weight. What weight did you wrestle at, anyway?"

"One sixty-five."

"You're a little heavier than that now, aren't you?"

"You bet! I hated having to starve myself!"

"But it made you mean and a winner!"

The dark young man, who bore a slight resemblance to Vida Blue, the baseball player, grinned modestly.

"You know why we're here, don't you?"

"Probably to ask me about the night Francine's parents were killed."

"That's right. Just tell me in your own words about that night."

"I don't know anything about the murders. When I heard about it I was scared to death!"

There was a note of sincerity in his voice that both officers believed.

"Go on."

"Francine and Cindy were here in the apartment. I left to go watch the Lakers game with my friend, Ron Hudson, and they went driving around, I guess. That's what they told me. When the game was over, I came back to the apartment and went to bed. It was early in the morning when Cindy crawled in bed with me, I didn't notice the time, but I do remember one thing. She squeezed my arm so tight, it made me mad, and I asked her, 'What's wrong with you?' And she said, 'I just love you so much, that's all.'"

Bartram wrote down the names of the people who might corroborate his story and they left.

"What do you think?"

"Well, of course, we have to check everything out, but I believe him." The detectives agreed that his story had the ring of truth, especially the part about Cindy crawling into bed and squeezing his arm so tight.

McGrath said slowly, "She must have been excited and maybe terrified, if she just witnessed two murders."

Bartram argued, "But why didn't she confide in someone?"

McGrath mused, "Maybe she knows who did it and is protecting them."

Two days after the murders, Stillwater residents were jumpy and nervous about the possible presence of homicidal killers in the area. South of the city, a water purifier salesman called on a farm family. While he was talking with the couple, the man excused himself for a moment and then came back to continue listening to the sales pitch.

"We kept him talking until you got here!" The farmer said, as a deputy sheriff drove up and got out of the car.

"I've been thrown off farms before, but this is a first! Calling the law on me." The salesman was obviously shaken.

"There's been a double murder in Stillwater, and people are understandably nervous. I'd suggest you ought to phone people first before you drive up to a place after dark, or maybe you might want to sell your stuff in a different area, until we catch the killer." After checking out his credentials and verifying that he was indeed a water purifier salesman, the deputy sheriff sent him on his way.

Relatives of the deceased couple arrived in town and began arranging the funeral. The Strode Funeral Home, owned by Bill Bernhardt, handled the services. Francine requested that her parents' bodies be cremated. Co-workers of the slain parents were saddened and huddled in little groups discussing the incredible event. Members of Jakey's Boys softball team that Mark and Dee Stepp belonged to were especially hard hit. They considered forfeiting the rest of the summer's games, but decided that the couple would have wanted them to carry on.

In most people's minds was the thought, "How could the murders have happened here? Houston, or Los Angeles, or Miami maybe, but not here!"

The police received one call concerning an older white GMC pickup truck. The only thing the driver was guilty of was driving with a bad muffler. There were no reports of blue key rings found.

The police had kept the crime scene both secured and under surveillance since the time of the murders. Francine asked Lieutenant Thrasher to allow her to obtain some clothing and shoes from the house. The lieutenant permitted Francine and her aunt, accompanied by an officer, to enter the sealed house.

"I'm going with you into the house and please do not touch anything in the residence without asking permission," the officer instructed them.

"I only want to go to my bedroom and get some stuff to wear," Francine said sourly.

"That's all right, but from the front door to the bedroom, please do not touch anything. I will be wearing gloves and if there is anything you need, point it out to me. I will open and close the doors for you."

The ladies obtained Francine's clothing and left. The barrier tape was still up at the residence, and a log was kept detailing each entry and exit from the crime scene.

The afternoon before the church service, the bodies of Mark and Dee Stepp were available for viewing in the State Room of the funeral home. The man and woman lying in the solid oak caskets were a handsome couple. They could have been sleeping. Preparing the bodies had not been easy, however, especially for the beautician, who was a friend of Dee's.

Debbie House, owner of the Greenery Beauty Salon, had received a phone call from Francine asking her to fix her mother's hair. Debbie had agreed and reported to the funeral home.

"It was one of the hardest things I've ever had to do." She was to tell friends later, "Walking down that long hallway, seeing Dee's body lying there on the gurney, I almost turned on my heel and left. We enjoyed such good times together! But I braced myself and did it, although tears were streaming down my cheeks all the time I was washing her hair and styling it."

The First Methodist Church on the corner of Duck and Seventh streets was the scene of the memorial service. It is a large parish of approximately eight hundred families and traces it beginnings back to before Oklahoma's statehood. The Methodists meet in a red brick structure built in the 1920s. The building has had several additions and remodeling jobs done, not all of them in the same style or matching brick. Both the Reverends, James Gragg and the youth minister Terry Martindale officiated. A member of the congregation sang *In the Garden* and *My Faith Looks Up to Thee*.

It is standard police procedure to monitor funerals, just as arson investigators study pictures of the crowds at fires. Experience has shown that sometimes the perpetrator will attend the funeral of his victim.

Oklahoma's heat wave had not abated and the temperature outside the air conditioned church was nearing one hundred degrees. Francine did not want to attend the funeral. She insisted that she would not go to the funeral. Her aunts were adamant that she must be there. They took her by the arms and almost forcibly helped her into the family car provided by the funeral home to drive from the motel where the family members were staying, to the church for the funeral. John C. Stepp, father of Mark Stepp, had flown down to the funeral from his home in Wisconsin. His wife Birdelle was in poor health. He was a white haired, down-to-earth type farmer that the Methodists and other townspeople warmed to at once. There were people in the congregation who were touched not only for the loss of their friends but to see the quiet dignity of the grieving old gentleman who had lost his son and daughter-in-law.

At last the funeral was over and the crowd dispersed. The bodies were taken to the crematorium. It would be another day before the Moose Lodge members would conduct the ceremony at the cemetery, where the ashes were interred. A motorcycle policeman preceded the funeral column, driving with their lights on, the first few cars with the purple and white flags attached denoting funeral procession. They drove to the Sunset Memorial Gardens cemetery, four miles south of Stillwater. There is a larger than life white statue of Jesus Christ. It is the only upright monument. All the graves are marked by flush stones, and there are flowers scattered here and there on the neatly trimmed green grass. A green awning and folding chairs provided by the funeral home marked the grave site.

After the ceremony, Francine's aunts took her with them to their motel room. Silent and composed throughout all the previous ceremonies, after the funeral, Francine threw herself across the bed at the motel and cried with heartbreaking sobs for almost an hour.

The aunts looked at each other with tenderness and relief. It was good for the girl to let her grief out. They had been worried by her unnatural calm.

The police had their hands full, trying to follow up and check out all the leads that were now coming into headquarters from the public.

An anonymous caller phoned to say that he was working with a man by the name of John James Warner, who was five feet ten inches tall, weighed one hundred eighty pounds with thinning brown hair and was clean shaven. According to the caller, Warner was currently on parole from murder in Tulsa County for shooting a homosexual. The caller said that when he asked Warner if he had heard about the murders, Warner gave him a cold stare, turned and walked off.

"Say, if this information turns out correct, this Warner guy lives in an apartment on North Perkins Road, almost walking distance from the Stepp house," McGrath pointed out to Bartram.

The investigators were momentarily buoyed with hope for a quick end to the solution of the murders. But the parolee had an alibi and no motive and they were forced to conclude that he was innocent.

In the news articles printed after the murders, the police were quoted as saying, "No weapon has been found, and there was nothing missing from the house."

A long-time friend and co-worker of Mark Stepp read the newspaper account and told his wife, "I know for a fact that Mark did own a .22 pistol. He even brought it to work one day, and I helped him clean it, disassemble it, and put it back together on our lunch hour."

"Then you've got to go to the police," his wife insisted.

"I don't understand why Francine didn't tell them her father had a gun. As close as the family was, I'm sure she knew it."

"You're not suspecting Francine!" His wife was horrified.

"Of course not! We've known her since she was just a little tyke, and Mark and Dee brought her to the softball games. I don't want to get her in trouble with the police, but I feel I ought to tell them about the gun."

He agonized over his decision to reveal his knowledge. Finally, he called Stillwater Police Headquarters. "I know that Mark Stepp owned a .22 caliber pistol," he told them.

A businesslike voice answered, "Thank you so much for the information. That's the third call we've had confirming the existence of a pistol in Mark Stepp's possession."

Francine was in police headquarters when Detective Bartram asked her about it. "We know your father had a pistol. Why didn't you mention it to us?"

Francine shrugged and folded her arms in front of her, in a characteristic gesture. Bartram waited in silence for a few moments and then inquired, "Why do you think these people told us there was a gun?"

Sullenly, "They might want to get me in trouble."

"Why should they want to do that?"

Again, the sour look and then silence. They replayed the scene several times, but Bartram could never get Francine to admit she knew there was a gun. As she left, she glanced back at the detective and it was obvious she bitterly resented him.

It was not long after that scene until the division commander had a visit from Francine's aunts. They were determined ladies in their mid-forties and told Lt. Thrasher they had come to complain.

"That detective, Billy Bartram, is like a rattlesnake!"

"Yes, he is! Lieutenant Thrasher, he acts like he's just coiled up getting ready to strike."

"And he's got no right to look at our niece that way! Why, that poor girl just cried her eyes out after the funeral the other day. We want to see Billy Bartram taken off this case!"

The lieutenant suppressed a smile at their description of Bartram. Slowly, he walked across the room, turned, and came back to the pair, "Ladies, look at it this way. If he can shake up innocent people with his stare, what must he do to people with a guilty conscience? Despite appearances, Bartram is one of my best men. We all want the same thing here and that's to find out who did this." The women departed, not much mollified by the lieutenant's explanation.

All over town, the murders were the topic of conversation. Many of the church congregations were exhorted to pray for the surviving relatives and for the swift accomplishment of justice. A woman at Mitzi Wynn's Wednesday night prayer service remarked that Mrs. Wynn had seemed especially distraught as she asked prayers for her daughter, that Cindy might gain God's forgiveness and pardon.

Cindy Wynn phoned the police again and asked to speak to Detective McGrath. They chatted for a while and then, "What would happen if a guy knew who killed them and didn't come forward?" Cindy hesitantly asked.

McGrath's pulse quickened, but he tried not to betray his excitement.

"If you know someone who knows something, you should give me his name. He could be charged with accessory after the fact, if he doesn't come forward."

"But what if he's scared to death? He's afraid he'll be killed himself."

"That's all the more reason to tell me who it is. We can keep him in protective custody."

"He's afraid, and he doesn't trust the police."

"Would he rather trust us, or people who have already killed twice? If you care about this friend of yours at all, you need to give me his name so we can protect him."

They continued sparring back and forth. Cindy hung up, saying, "I'll think about it."

In the meantime, the police received an anonymous tip that a Jeff Adams was into Satanism and might be involved.

"What do you think?" Dennis McGrath was asking Billy Bartram. "Do you know this Adams kid?"

"I think the worst thing he's done is wear his hair spiked and dress weird so people are afraid of him, but I guess we'll have to check it out."

They decided to call on Adams. He was not in Chicago's, the bar where he was known to hang out, but the lawmen were told where Adams might be found. They went to the dimly lit Murphy's bar and found him.

The most striking feature of the young man was the hair standing straight up about six inches from the top of his head and cut off, resembling a stiff bristled brush. He had three earrings in one ear and a shirt-tail that reached the knees of his baggy pants. Two high topped tennis shoes of different colors, untied, completed his apparel.

"What were you doing in the Stepps' neighborhood the night they were killed?"

"I was worried about Francine, so I went by, but she wasn't home."

"We heard you are really into *Dungeons and Dragons*."

"I used to be, about five years ago, but I haven't played in a long time now."

"What do you know about a group called the Bats?"

"Is that a new rock group, or what?" Adams smiled.

"Just tell us where you were the night of the murders."

"Well, I was in Chicago's most of the evening, then I left there with some friends and went to Murphy's."

The officers took down the names of witnesses that might corroborate his whereabouts and left. "What do you think?" McGrath asked, driving away.

"Basically, despite his punk garb, I think he's harmless, but we'll check him out and see if anyone in the group noticed he was absent for awhile."

"He would have had to change clothes, if he slipped away from his friends and went to the house, murdered them and then went back and joined them again. Someone should have noticed if he was gone long enough to do all that."

"Plus he has no motive."

"I thought Satanists didn't have to have motives."

"Actually, I doubt the boy is half as bad as he'd like his parents to believe. My guess is he mostly enjoys shocking them."

A call came into the station from Cindy Wynn for McGrath. They played sparring games for awhile. "All right, the one who knows about the murders is John Biggsley," she finally told him. "I'll try to find him and tell him what you said, but he may have already left the state." And she hung up the phone quickly.

"Hallelujah! A break at last."

When no phone calls or contact came in from Biggsley, McGrath and Bartram proceeded to do the legwork that makes up most of the policeman's routine. They called the high school and talked with Dr. Merritt, the principal, and discovered that Biggsley had gone to school with both Francine and Cindy and had recently enlisted in the Air Force.

They learned that he was stationed in Alexandria, Louisiana. McGrath contacted the Special Investigations department of Tinker Air Force Base in Oklahoma City. He found out that Biggsley was assigned to an Equipment Maintenance Squadron at England AFB. The lieutenant authorized a trip to see Biggsley. "You better take your polygraph equipment with you."

McGrath and Bartram loaded a suitcase full of equipment into a small four seater airplane, piloted by Greg Nash. Lieutenant Taylor rode along as co-pilot, in case they needed an instrument rated pilot. It was clear flying across Arkansas and the men remarked on the beauty of the green forest-covered hills. They saw the muddy Mississippi below them as they neared Louisiana and their destination. They were met by Special Agent Allen Smith, who directed them to the Air Force Office of Special Investigations office and briefed the officers in charge, including Biggsley's First Sergeant, on the nature of the case. It was only a few minutes until Airman Bales marched in.

"Are you acquainted with John Biggsley?"

"Yes, sir, I am."

"How well do you know him?"

"Pretty well. We go out together sometimes."

"Have you ever known him to be violent?"

"Never. He may be a little weird, but he's certainly not violent."

"Have you ever seen him with a knife?"

"No, sir. I've never seen him with a knife or a gun."

"You know that we are investigating a homicide that occurred on the night of June 7."

"I don't think he would ever be involved in a homicide, and as far as I know Biggsley has never been AWOL."

Bales was dismissed then and an Airman Borrow presented himself. The sergeant had told them that Borrow was native of Louisiana and a good recruit. He had dark eyes and a frank, open countenance.

"We understand that you are Biggsley's roommate."

"That is correct, sir."

"How well do you know Biggsley?"

"Not very well. We work different shifts, we have different interests and we never go out socially together."

"In other words, you don't like the guy."

"I wouldn't say that exactly." There was a pause while the airman searched for words. "He's just a little weird, that's all."

"What do you mean by weird?"

"I can't explain it. It's just something I feel, you know, just a gut feeling. He doesn't react to things the way you expect him to."

"Was he present in your barracks the night of June 7?"

"Well, he should have been. I can't be positive, but I think so."

Borrow was dismissed and John Biggsley, possible suspect, or witness marched into the room. Bartram was studying the recruit. He was blonde, with his hair cut close to the scalp. He was quite obviously nervous and he picked at his face where a few pimples revealed his youthfulness. There was something familiar about him.

"Now, do you know why we're here?"

Biggsley tried to talk, but had to clear his throat before he could get the words out. "It's something to do with two people who got murdered in Stillwater, but I don't know anything about it, honest!"

"Sometimes people know things that they don't realize are important. We'll start out by me asking you some questions and you just answer by telling me the truth and we'll be out of here before you know it."

Specialist First Class Biggsley admitted that he knew Cindy Wynn, Francine Stepp and Jeff Adams, but he denied any knowledge of or involvement in the killings.

The day wore on. At one point, Biggsley suddenly blurted out, "I know you! You arrested me on the Strip once," the Strip being the street closest to OSU Campus that has a number of beer joints on it.

"That's right! It was about some fraternity vandalism. You look a little different than you did then." Privately, Bartram was remembering him dressed as a punk rocker—quite a change from the uniform today.

"Obviously I don't always agree with the establishment viewpoint," the young airman admitted.

"When was the last time you were in Stillwater?"

"That would be around April 18, when I was on leave."

"Where did you stay when you were in Stillwater?"

"I stayed in a dorm on the OSU campus."

"At that time did you have occasion to talk with Francine Stepp or her parents?"

"I called Francine on the phone and we talked for a half hour. Maybe an hour."

"Her father was shot and stabbed, and her mother was stabbed to death at their home. Do you have any ideas on that?"

"I don't want to get anyone in trouble, but the only person I can think of would be Jeff Adams. I've seen him get violent. I've even seen him carve himself with a knife and draw pictures of people killed by knives, and I think he's sort of crazy."

They continued talking about the murders. Bartram was convinced the kid was telling the truth, but he thought he would show him the picture of the knife used to stab Dee Stepp. He had carefully concealed the part of the picture showing Dee's body. Only the knife handle, enlarged to show the wooden handle and the three brass rivets that held the blade, was observable in the picture.

Bartram threw the picture down on the table. "Do you know anything about a knife like that?"

Biggsley's face paled and he pushed back away from the table, crossed his arms in front of him and refused to answer any more questions.

Finally, they decided that further questioning was useless, so he was dismissed.

The lawmen discussed the problem with the Special Agent. "We've determined from the records kept here that he could not have physically done the murders, but he knows something."

"The picture of that knife sure spooked him! I wish we could get him to talk more."

The men flew back to Oklahoma in the evening. They were too tired and discouraged to notice the glorious sunset. They had left Stillwater with high hopes for a break to solve the case, and they were returning with nothing.

It was to be a pattern that dogged them through the weeks of working on the Stepp case.

Chapter Three

The summer heat blanketed the state. Every weather forecaster agreed that there were no signs of rain to break the drought. Climbing into a patrol car was like entering a super heated plastic torture chamber. Bartram angled the air conditioning vents to blow the cool air on his face, realizing that his shirt was stuck to the back of the seat already.

McGrath said, "I wish they wouldn't put the temperature on the bank clock sign. You're better off not knowing how hot it is."

Bartram nodded. This was a routine follow-up after the Biggsley questioning. Both Bartram and McGrath were taking a longer look at Jeff Adams, the weird-dressing suspected Satanist who was a friend of Francine's.

They questioned witnesses, classmates, and the persons who could provide Adams with an alibi for the time of the murders.

Glad to return to the cooler haven of Headquarters, the two lawmen went over the information they had received.

"Do you think we ought to call Adams down here and ask him some more questions?" McGrath wondered.

"He's the best lead we have so far. I'm going to give his folks a call and ask him to come in voluntarily." Bartram picked up the phone.

It was not long before the youth sauntered into the station. He appeared as he normally did, with spiked hair, wearing three earrings and an over-sized long-tailed shirt. Despite his punk apparel, he seemed mild and agreeable when asked to sign a body waiver.

Bartram explained, "We need your permission to obtain a few hair samples from you, a little blood, and we'd also like to get your fingerprints and palm prints."

"Why not? You want to take my picture again?" Adams grinned at them.

"No, but we would like to talk with you about the evening that the Stepps were killed. Just start at the beginning and tell us everything you can remember from that evening."

Adams shrugged. "It was no different than any other evening. Let me see, I ate dinner with my folks. Then I went to Chicago's. I called Francine, and like I told you, nobody answered. We sat around, drank a few beers, shot a few games of pool, just hanging out, you know. It was no big deal."

"What time did you drive by Francine's house?" Bartram asked him, intently studying the young man's face. "We have witnesses who can place your car in the neighborhood, so you might as well level with us."

Adams looked skeptical, "Well, your witnesses can tell you I went up to the door, rang the bell, nobody answered, so I went away. I got witnesses, too, you know. And I don't know exactly what time it was, I don't do everything by no damn clock."

"Did you hate Mark and Delores Stepp?" McGrath watched to see Adams reaction as he threw the unexpected question at him.

"Hell, no! I know they were giving Francine a hard time, but they never fucked with me. Nobody fucks with me, get that!" Adams suddenly changed from the agreeable young man to a grimly angry young man.

Bartram and McGrath did not look at each other, but they were both thinking the mercurial change of mood was significant.

"We'd like you to take a polygraph test." Bartram explained that his consent was needed and that, if he failed the test, the results could not be used in a court of law, but if he passed it the law officers would consider the results valid and would probably cease calling on him and questioning him.

"Sure, why not. I got nothing to hide." Adams sounded belligerent, but confident.

Adams passed the polygraph test. That fact, plus the statements of witnesses who accounted for his whereabouts during the crucial time of the murders, made the officers realize they had been on a false trail.

The next day at police headquarters, Bartram was talking with McGrath "Let's run through this crime scene again. Maybe we can get a handle on what happened by examining what we do know from the evidence."

McGrath nodded. "Okay. Where do you want to start?"

"The evening of the crime. Here's two people that have to get up and go to work the next day. They just got home from the trip to Kansas and Mark mows the lawn."

McGrath picks up the tale, "And we know from the clothes hung to drip dry that Dee did laundry that day."

"Right. They eat supper and take a bottle of wine to the bedroom with them."

"Do we know if that was routine for them?"

"From the empty beer cartons and wine cooler cartons it seems they enjoyed a drink to relax. Nothing unusual about that."

"So far, everything is a perfectly normal evening. Then we get into the discrepancies. Did Francine ask permission to spend the night with Cindy? You saw the excuses scratched off the list, like Francine was afraid to ask them and wanted to have her explanations ready."

"Cindy says she never talked to the parents," McGrath reminded Bartram.

"Okay, for a moment, let's assume Francine asked and got permission to spend the night with Cindy. They leave and the couple goes to bed to sleep."

"We know from the condition of the doorway that the bedroom door was kicked open."

"Wouldn't your first reaction be to sit up in bed? You wouldn't automatically jump out of bed, would you?"

"No way, especially if you just drifted off into deep slumber. Plus, they may have been a little woozy from the wine they'd drunk."

"So you sit up in bed and see someone pointing a gun at you." Bartram stood in the doorway and held his hands in front of him, simulating a shooting stance. McGrath was across the room and assumed a sitting position.

"Now, what would you do next? Scream? Jump up out of bed? Reach for the telephone?"

"We don't know the exact sequence of things and the Stepps sure can't tell us, but I suspect the gun shots were next."

"If Dee turned to her husband and saw the blood from his neck wound, that could have caused her to delay a few seconds."

"A few fatal seconds for her." McGrath remarked somberly. "It could have delayed her getting help by using the phone."

"Remember the phone in the kitchen was jerked out." The men pondered that. They both knew that burglars rarely enter a house where they know people are sleeping. "It could have been a drug hit, but there is absolutely no evidence that either of the Stepps were ever involved in any kind of drug use, let alone drug trafficking."

"What about the wrong house, wrong people theory?"

"That could be, but we've got no suspicious individuals in the neighborhood." The officers considered what they knew of the residents of the area.

Shaking his head, Bartram continued, "Okay, your husband has just been shot and the killer is advancing on you with a knife in his hand. What do you do?"

"I grab for the telephone." McGrath reaches out, simulating Dee's actions.

Bartram advances, hand held high in pretense of a knife-wielder. "I stab you at the same time I wrestle for the telephone, ripping it from your hand."

"And I try to escape being stabbed by running around the bed. Why don't I escape by running out into the hallway?"

"Because our second assailant is guarding that door with another gun or knife, or simply standing there, blocking the door."

"So," McGrath continues, crouching to avoid the onslaught of the knife. "Now I am unable to get away. There's a bed on one side, the dresser on the other side, and the wall at my back. To get away from the knife, I turn my back on you."

"And I finish you off this way!" Bartram pushing his hand in against McGrath's lower rib cage.

"Hmmm. What did we learn by this little exercise?"

"That the assailants weren't very good shots, for one thing. Four bullets went wild. That could mean they were high on drugs."

"Or it could mean they weren't familiar with firearms."

"I'd say we've pretty well established that there had to be two persons involved, otherwise Delores Stepp could have run out the doorway and maybe gotten away."

"Yeah, remember that fellow Johnson who was knifed and left a trail of blood down Washington Street? They sewed him up and he recovered. It's pretty amazing what doctors can do."

"Somebody wanted these people dead. They weren't just stabbed once or twice. These killers made sure they were dead. What did they do to earn that kind of death?"

"Maybe the murderers belonged to a Satanic cult."

"We haven't found any evidence of that yet. But let's take it from a different angle. The killers are covered in blood. They had to be! Now why is it we haven't found any bloody clothing, or why hasn't anyone come forward to say they saw two people in blood-splattered clothing?"

"Either no one saw them, or they could be transients who are in another state by now and we're beating our heads against a stone wall."

"The city sanitation works were advised to let us know if they retrieved any bloody clothing from the trash dumpsters."

McGrath and Bartram continued discussing the case. Although they tried to bolster each other's spirits, they both had the sinking feeling that the Stepp murders might join the list of unsolved crimes. They were not aware they would soon receive their first break in the case.

There were persistent rumors told to individual policemen that a boy had overheard the assailants plotting the crime, but the police dismissed it as one more unreliable bit of gossip circulating around town.

Then a phone call came into police headquarters. A man identified himself as the manager of a fast food restaurant. "One of my cooks says he overheard two girls planning to murder their parents, and he thought it was a joke, until this happened. I think you might want to send someone around to question him."

The information was duly recorded and Bartram and McGrath went out to interview the witness. He lived with his father and stepmother in a white house close to the Main Street of Stillwater in an older section of town. The structure was well kept. Next door, a two story house had a washing machine and an old television set on the porch and two cars up on blocks.

The witness was a tall young man with sandy brown hair, a pleasant smile and a nervous stutter.

"Hello, Mike. I'm Dennis McGrath and this is Billy Bartram. You can call me Dennis. We're investigating the murders of Mark and Delores Stepp and we need all the help we can get. We'd like you to tell us what you know."

"I don't know nothing about the murders."

"Okay. But we know you've been telling people at work that you overheard two girls talking about killing their parents."

"Well, mostly it was Cindy Wynn doing the talking. Francine just sorta sat there."

"Was there anyone else there?"

"Do you mean the first time they talked about it or the second time?"

The officers glanced at each other. This was incredible!

"Just tell us about the first time. Where were you when you heard them talking."

"At my house."

"And what was Cindy Wynn and Francine Stepp doing there?"

"Cindy was living with my folks when I first come down here from Arkansas, and Francine was her best friend, so she was over at the house a lot."

"And was there anyone else there?"

"Uh-huh. Jackie Myers was there. He was just laying on the floor, listening, he didn't say nothing."

"What did they say when you came into the room."

"They said 'Hi'"

"And then what happened?"

"I said, 'Hi' and went over and sat down."

"Go on."

"Cindy and Francine was talking about getting rid of Francine's parents, 'cause they wouldn't let Cindy hang around with her and go out with her and stuff like that."

"And how long did they talk about getting rid of her parents?"

"About thirty minutes. They offered Jackie a whole lot of money to get rid of her parents, but he wasn't interested."

"How much money?"

"I don't remember, but it was a lot, I remember that."

"Then what happened?"

"I got up to take a shower, and that's all I heard."

"Did you worry about it? Did you think about calling the police or trying to warn her parents?"

"No. I didn't think they meant it. Everybody blows off steam and says things they don't mean. They was mad. I figured they would get over it."

"You mentioned that you overheard them talking about 'getting rid of Francine's parents' a second time. When was that?"

"I don't know the exact day. It was a few days after the first time."

"And what did you hear that time?"

"Cindy wanted to know where she could find a gun."

The officers were careful not to look at each other. They were excited at what they were hearing, but they remained outwardly calm.

"Who was in the room with you that time?"

"Just Cindy, Francine and me. My stepbrother walked through the room once but he didn't stay."

"Did you think they were serious when they were talking about getting rid of Francine's parents?"

"No. I thought they was blowing off steam. I took it as a big joke."

"What else did they say that day?"

"Just that they was going to go in and do it and they was going to send Francine back in a few hours later and she was going to play it off like nothing happened."

"Did you tell anyone about what the girls said?"

"Not 'til after it happened. Then I told my dad, and my manager and Eric, the day cook and Ricky, the closer at the store, and Vince, general manager and Kim the breakfast manager. And I talked to my mom."

The detectives were making notes while Mike was talking. Then they told him, "You realize we may have to ask you to testify under oath about this."

The young man shrugged, with an unhappy look on his face.

As they drove away, Bartram commented to McGrath, "In that small house you wouldn't think his parents would be renting rooms to runaways."

"Yes, but they do that, quite frequently."

Both officers were acquainted with Jackie Myers. He was a slender, dark haired youth with a mustache and was regarded by the cops as a punk. Seldom employed, he was known to brag about how tough he was, but the police had never caught him in anything seriously criminal. The first time they went out to call on him he wasn't home and they talked with his mother. She told them when she expected Jackie to return.

On the second call he opened the door warily. "What do you want?"

"We can ask the questions here or downtown, Jackie."

"Okay, come on in."

"We want you to tell us what you know about the Stepp murders."

The youth didn't say anything for a moment. He stared at the floor, then glanced around the room, finally facing the cops with an angry stare.

"That dumb Mike has been talking to you, hasn't he?"

"Just tell us what you know, Jackie. You realize we're going to find out the truth sooner or later, anyway."

"I thought they was kidding."

"You thought who was kidding?"

"Cindy and Francine. They offered me fifty-thousand dollars to get rid of Francine's parents."

"Where were they going to get that kind of money?"

"I dunno. They said something about life insurance, but I didn't believe 'em."

"Okay. Now where and when did this conversation take place?"

"I don't remember what day it was. We was all over at Mike's house when they was talking about it."

"Can you try to remember what day of the week it was? Or was it around some holiday, or something to help us fix the time?"

"I dunno. Ask Mike. He heard the same thing. He was sittin' in a chair the whole time they was talking about it."

"Did you tell anyone about this conversation?"

"What do you think, I'm stupid or somethin'? I didn't say nothing to nobody!"

The officers asked a few more questions, making notes of the conversation and told him he might be subpoenaed later, to give his statement under oath.

Jackie gave them a squint-eyed stare that Bartram thought he'd copied from watching Clint Eastwood and Chuck Norris films, and the officers left.

"What do you think?"

"It has the ring of truth to me. I can't visualize either one of those boys as being jilted boyfriends with a motive for revenge, can you?"

"No. And especially that Mike Reed. He told everybody he worked with, but you can tell he's scared of going to court."

The next day McGrath and Bartram interviewed Mike Reed's father. He told them he hadn't heard either of the conversations his son had reported to them. Then he added, thoughtfully, "It was about three weeks before the deaths that Cindy asked me where she could get a silencer for a gun."

"Did she say what type of gun it was?"

"No. I told her that a blanket, a pillow or some steel wool would do the same thing."

"Didn't that seem kind of strange to you? Cindy asking about a silencer, I mean?"

"Oh, you know how these kids are. Half the time I don't pay no attention to what they say."

The officers thanked him for his help and left.

"I think it's time we paid a call on Cindy Wynn's parents, don't you?"

Mitzi Wynn was mowing the lawn when they drove out to the Rogers neighborhood. She was of average height, brown hair, wearing a tank top and shorts. She shut off the lawnmower and they moved to the two-car garage attached to the house, where they could talk.

"It's so hot today!" Mitzi Wynn mopped her brow and fanned herself. The lawmen observed that the house was somewhat similar to the Stepps' house. It appeared to be a comfortable, well kept home. Mitzi was nervously rolling up a garden hose and tidying the neat garage.

"We're here to ask you a few questions about your daughter, Mrs. Wynn."

Her face fell, as though a dark cloud passed over it. "Cindy is my stepdaughter, officers."

"We understand that she moved out of your house here when she was only seventeen."

"Yes, she did. She's always hated me for taking her father away from her. Cindy has deliberately tried to make my life miserable. If she could get back at me she would do it. The saddest part is that the person she hurts the most, next to herself, of course, is her father."

"We have some witnesses who are ready to swear that

Cindy was involved in planning to get rid of Francine's parents."

Tears came to her eyes and she whispered, "I asked my husband the morning of the murders what he would do if his daughter was involved and he said, "We'll cross that bridge when we come to it."

The detectives thought it significant that neither parent doubted she was capable of planning the crime.

"Were you close friends with Dee Stepp?"

"I knew her, of course, because of the girls, but I wouldn't say anyone was really *close* to Dee. She was a very private person, but at the same time she was very outspoken, if that makes any sense to you."

"When you talked with her, did she ever seem worried about her daughter?"

"Oh, no. Dee was very proud of Francine. She would never admit it, if they had a problem. I may have made a mistake, but I told her months ago that Cindy was a bad influence and they shouldn't let Francine run around with her. She would pick up bad habits."

"Did they follow your advice?"

"They tried, but I knew the girls were slipping around, seeing each other. I even heard that Francine was dating a black boy for awhile. If Dee and Mark had known about it they would have been furious."

"We have heard from other sources that Francine and her parents had a big argument, shouting and screaming, shortly before the murders."

Mitzi nodded her head sadly. "I'd talked with Dee and told her the girls were still running around together and she was determined to put her foot down."

The officers thanked her for her cooperation and left.

Cindy Wynn called the police department to talk with McGrath. She told him, "Francine and her boyfriend came over to my house after the murders and we were sitting on the steps in the hallway. Francine had some scratches on her left arm and I asked her where she got them and she said she got them during a fight with her mother. I didn't want to tell you this, but I thought you should know."

McGrath hung up the phone and sighed, "Billy, it looks like we've got to go talk with Francine's boyfriend again."

Bartram and McGrath drove to Perkins to interview Fred. He had gotten off work and was at his parents' house. While he didn't seem glad to see them, he didn't glare at them, either. He heaved a sigh when he opened the door, inviting them inside.

"We need to ask you a few more things, Fred. The morning of June 8, when Francine called you, what exactly did she say?"

"Just that her parents were dead."

"Do you think it is possible that she could have killed her parents?"

"No way! When I swat a fly she walks out of the room and screams."

"Now, how do you usually spend your evenings?"

"I'm usually with Francine. Sometimes we go to the show, and sometimes we just drive around Boomer Lake."

"Have you known her to spend the night with Cindy before?"

"No."

"Why do you think Francine didn't want you around the night of June 7?"

"Well, I had to get up and go to work at six o'clock the next morning."

"What was your relationship with Francine? Were you planning on getting married?"

"Yes, we were. We were talking about getting married on the weekend of June 11-12. Francine was going to be with me when we talked to her parents about it."

"Did Francine ever mention her parent's life insurance policies to you?"

"Yes, she did, but that doesn't prove anything."

"We've heard rumors about Francine dating a black male. Do you know anything about that?"

"She told me that there was this black guy that she used to play pool with and he raped her. He's in prison now."

"Now, back to the evening of June 7. Francine and Cindy mentioned taking some aluminum cans south of town and selling them for spending money."

"They took some cans to sell all right, but it was on Tuesday morning."

"Did you know Francine's parents were nudists?"

"Not until all this happened, and it came out in the newspapers. Francine told me she didn't participate in that, anyway."

"You were aware that Francine went with her parents to Kansas?"

"Yes, they went in the Chevy."

"What do you know about the Trans Am? Who drives it?"

"Francine's mother. She was very protective of that car. If it was going to rain she had that car inside!"

The detectives concluded their interviews with Fred. Driving back to Stillwater, they discussed him. "He seems like a good kid. I think Francine was using him as a patsy."

"Funny, she never said anything before about a black guy raping her and we haven't found anyone else that heard anything about it."

"I believe that like I believe she didn't take her clothes off when she went to the nudist camp."

"These girls have a chronic problem with the truth. Even little things, like what time of day did they go to sell aluminum cans—they can't get their stories straight."

Bartram concluded, "I think it's time we got Francine, Cindy and Fred to take polygraph tests."

The prosecution is barred from using polygraph tests in a court of law to prosecute cases, but defense attorneys may introduce them if the findings are favorable. It would seem contradictory that the police would be in favor of polygraph tests, however, many lawmen believe the tests are more reliable than the general public has been led to believe. In rare instances are perpetrators able to confuse and mislead the experienced polygraph operator.

Fred Rank appeared to have no knowledge and no complicity in the murder case, according to the polygraph examiner. The results of Francine's and Cindy's polygraph examination was not made public to the police.

At headquarters the lieutenant informed Bartram and McGrath that he was going to request a search warrant and that he had contacted Oklahoma State Bureau of Investigation for a specialist to come to Stillwater. The officer would conduct a presumptive test for invisible traces of blood using the chemical Luminol.

Then it was evening and time for Bartram and McGrath to accompany Officer Mary M. Long from OSBI to the crime scene and help conduct the search. Luminol is a chemical used by investigative personnel in liquid form that is sprayed from a bottle, looking much like a Windex glass cleaner bottle. Even traces of blood that have been washed off and are too minutely diluted for the naked eye to see will glow phosphorescent in the presence of blood and the absence of light. That is why the search was conducted at ten-thirty p.m. and why windows and openings were taped to prevent street lights from shining in. Each of the officers wore plastic coverings over their shoes and gloves to keep from contaminating evidence.

Standing just outside the darkened house, in the entryway, Bartram whispered to his buddy, "I don't mind telling you the hairs on the back of my neck are standing straight up."

On the inside doorknob of the front door were bloody traces. The carpet was sprayed from the front door in toward the kitchen area. Visible before the officers, glowing eerily greenish were two types of footprints. The ones by the door were slim and appeared to be somewhat smeared. The prints found in the area around the kitchen and family room were larger. The outlines of the bloody footprints were too indistinct to confirm a particular shoe style or size. The master bedroom showed vast amounts of blood, but nothing there contributed to the evidence in the case, although it was obvious the blood on the soles of the killers' feet was tracked from the master bedroom to the patio door and then out the front door. The officers were somewhat surprised that the assailants did not track blood outside the patio door onto the concrete patio, but they had not.

There was no blood on the stairway, confirming what the police had already determined—that the killers hadn't gone upstairs.

They continued their examination of the downstairs. "Look at that!" McGrath pointed out the area in front of the patio door. From the marks in the area, it appeared the perpetrators had wiped their bloody feet off at the doorway.

Spraying the kitchen area and bar countertop nearest the telephone, revealed a perfect palm print. It was sprayed with Ortho-tolledene, a hazardous substance, to preserve it. Then Bartram saved the palm print for evidence by removing part of the kitchen counter.

Then Officer Long sprayed the clear glass patio door. Toward the bottom of the door were blood stains, but it was at elbow height that they saw several fingerprints with their distinctive ridges and whorls.

"Voila! It looks like a perfect print!"

There were congratulations all around. They felt they were making progress on the case. Quickly, the area was sprayed with the chemical to preserve it. The print was photographed for enlargement and examination by the OSBI fingerprint experts.

Around them the gloomy residence seemed to smell of evil and sudden, violent death. The officers closed the door on the silent, darkened house and if they walked a little hastily to their cars, it is understandable.

The next day Police Headquarters was visited by a brother of the victim. He spoke to Lt. Thrasher and inquired if an arrest had been made. He was told the investigation was continuing.

He told them that an attorney had been retained to handle the Stepp estate and that Francine's grandfather had been appointed executor. He had helped Francine open a checking account with money provided by the grandfather and he had taken Francine to apply for Social Security benefits.

The lieutenant asked him what the family's plans were.
"I'm going back home, and so is my father. Francine is going to spend a week in Kansas with her relatives there and then possibly visit her grandmother."

"We'd like to be advised when Francine leaves town and she needs to provide us with her current address with relatives. We might need to contact her in a hurry if we get a break on this case."

"I'll certainly do that."

Bartram had already been phoned by Francine's aunt and told that they had found the key to Mark and Dee's safety deposit box and that they had destroyed Mark and Dee's bank access cards, to prevent anyone from unlawfully using them.

He spoke to his partner, "Looks like she's going to be a well-to-do orphan. I'm going to call her and ask about those scratches on her arms that Cindy mentioned."

"Francine, Cindy tells us that you had some scratches on your arms after the murder and she said you told her they were from getting in a fight with your mother."

"I don't know why she would say that."

"Well, why do you think she would say that?"

"Just to get me in trouble."

Bartram thought privately that was Francine's answer to every discrepancy—someone was trying to get her in trouble. She continued denying she had ever had any scratches on her arm or that she had made that statement to Cindy.

The official responsible for processing the paper work of the O.G.& E. employees life insurance policies had been summoned to the attorney's office while Francine's relatives were in town to explain the death benefits of the policies.

Glenn Rowland, O.G.& E. employee had known Mark Stepp and liked him well. He hadn't played on the softball team with Mark, but he'd heard what a good pitcher and excellent athlete he was. He knew Mark was regarded highly by his co-workers and team members, especially because he pulled his weight at work and if the team lost a game, he didn't get moody about it, but accepted defeat with good grace and a laugh. Rowland dreaded the emotional scene that he anticipated at the attorney's office. He knew the family's reputation for being very close and he didn't know how he would handle a hysterical young woman.

Upon his return to the Sooner Generating Station, he was asked by several persons who knew the purpose of his errand how it went.

"I couldn't believe it, at first, but now I think Francine had something to do with the murders. She was so calm and dry-eyed as we were talking about her parents' deaths and what they wanted and planned for her. I can't help believing that she is somehow involved in their deaths."

The call came into Police Headquarters from the Oklahoma State Bureau of Investigation.

"We've got a match on the fingerprints on the glass sliding door. They belong to Francine Stepp."

Bartram and McGrath conferred with Lieutenant Thrasher.

"That nails it! We have witnesses that overheard them plotting the crime and now her bloody fingerprints turn up! Francine swore that when she returned the morning of June 8, she didn't touch anything in the bedroom. She just saw that her parents were dead and ran next door." The lieutenant was eager to wrap up the case, but he hesitated for a moment, reviewing the events in the case.

"Let's go over what we have here." He looked at the detectives. "We have the girls' own discrepancies on times and whether they saw the parents alive that evening," Bartram pointed out.

"We have motive, and now we have some facts to back up our suspicions," McGrath added.

"If we could only persuade them to tell us where they disposed of the gun, that would really tie up the case," Thrasher mused.

"Bartram, why don't you call the aunt and tell her we'd like Francine to come in for questioning? But be sure to emphasize that it is just a request. We are not ordering her to come in."

The men waited with suspense for Francine's appearance. They wanted to see her face when they told her that her fingerprint in blood had been found on the glass patio door.

Francine appeared at the station with her aunt and grandfather. She was composed, as usual, unsmiling and calm. Her aunt and grandfather appeared tired from the strain of the last few days.

"Would you like to come into my office, Francine? I'd like to speak to you alone." Bartram waited, and Francine shrugged and walked into his office. She sat down, facing him across the desk, but kept her face averted.

"If you want to leave at any time, you are free to do so. I am not arresting you. I want you to realize that. I just want to talk with you and explain to you the strength of the evidence that is accumulating against you." Bartram summarized the information they had. He told her about the witnesses who had heard her planning the murders, the attempt to find a gun and learn about a silencer, the proposition to a witness to pay him to get rid of her parents, plus the new item that her bloody fingerprints had been found.

"I don't know anything about that. They are lying," Francine said, sullenly.

"If you're not going to tell me the truth, you might as well leave." Bartram was exasperated at his inability to reach her. Francine threw him a look of loathing and got up and flounced out of the room.

Bartram spoke to the lieutenant. "I'm not getting anywhere with Francine."

Lieutenant Thrasher thought for a moment. "Ask her aunt and grandfather to come up to my office, without Francine."

They complied with his request, and as they seated themselves across from him, Lieutenant Thrasher felt sorrow at the additional grief he was going to inflict. Looking at their sad eyes, he wondered if they hadn't already suspected the truth.

As gently as he could, he enumerated the evidence that the police had discovered. He covered the whole range of their investigation, and concluded by saying, "We have enough items now to bring charges against Francine. What we would like to do is gain her cooperation. If she would tell us all she knows, it would be better. She is a very troubled young woman, I think you know that. In fact, you may have suspected she was responsible."

It was a time of sorrowing for the relatives. Then they dried their eyes. "I'll talk to Francine," the aunt said.

Francine and her aunt were closeted in a room for a while, and both women shed tears, but the aunt came out and shook her head at the policemen, saying, "She won't talk to me about it."

Then it was the grandfather's turn. His deep bass voice carried through the thin walls of the detectives' room. The officers waiting outside could hear the warmth and love in his voice as he spoke to her.

"Francine, you know that I love you."

"And I love you, grandpa," Francine quietly responded.

"Have I ever lied to you?"

"No, you haven't."

"Well, I'm not lying to you now. You need help, and the only way you're going to get that help is to tell them all you know about it."

There were the sounds of weeping from the room, and awhile later, the old gentleman came out. "She'll talk to you now," he told the lieutenant.

Lieutenant Thrasher started by asking Francine where the weapon was.

She told him that they had thrown the pistol into Boomer Lake by the dam. He got out a map, and Francine marked it with an X at the approximate location where they had thrown the gun.

Then the lieutenant handed Francine the Miranda warning on a card and she held it while he read it to her. He had her initial the corner of it with the date. He explained that her statement would be recorded by video camera.

"We planned that morning to kill my parents," Francine told him. "I got the gun from the bedroom in the afternoon. The way we planned it, I was supposed to kick the bedroom door open and Cindy Wynn was supposed to shoot them. When we got to the bedroom door, Cindy handed me the gun and said she was scared. We went back down the hall, and I was still holding the gun. I asked her what she was doing and Cindy said , 'It is now or never.' We went back down the hall, and Cindy kicked open the door and the gun went off."

"The gun that was in your hand?"

"Yes. The gun just kept going off and it scared me. I went into the kitchen and got a knife and went back to the bedroom."

"What was your mother doing while you went to get the knife?"

"I don't know."

"Where was Cindy?"

"She went outside."

"Did you stab your mother?"

"I don't know. I don't remember much after the gun going off."

"Then what did you do?"

"We put the gun in a bag and drove over the dam and Cindy threw it in the lake."

McGrath drove out to Randall Jackson's apartment to pick up Cindy Wynn. He brought her to the police headquarters. She was handed the Miranda warning as it was read to her and she initialed and dated it.

"Now, we want you to tell us your full involvement in the murder of Francine's parents."

"Dennis, I don't know anything about it." Cindy could still smile at McGrath playfully.

"We have Francine in a room across the hall and she has already told us what happened."

There was a split second when McGrath thought she was going to continue to deny everything, but then he saw she correctly interpreted his statement as the truth. He could see she was stunned for a moment to learn Francine had confessed. Then she started sobbing and crying. Finally, when she composed herself she began her statement, also before a video camera.

"I didn't know Francine was really going to shoot them! Francine had talked to me earlier that day about killing her parents and I told her, 'Francine you're crazy.' That evening, after my boyfriend left, Francine picked me up and we came over to her house and she showed me a gun. I asked her what it was for and she said, 'To do what needed to be done.' She told me to kick in their door, so I did and hollered out their names. They sat up in bed and Francine started shooting. I ran outside, screaming, 'No, Francine! Oh, God!' Then a little later, Francine came out and told me to quit screaming or she was going to kill me next. I was quiet then. Then Francine told me to come back in the house because she needed to finish off her mother. I waited in the living room. Then I peeped around the corner and saw what Francine was doing. She was bent over her mother stabbing her. Then she said, 'Let's go.'"

"Francine made me drive her to the South Main Laundromat. She stripped to her underwear and washed and dried her clothes. Then she made me take her back to Randy's place. I was scared to tell anyone, because Francine told me she would kill me if I told anyone."

At the conclusion of this statement, Francine Stepp and Cindy Wynn were placed under arrest for first degree murder and booked into the municipal jail. Charges were signed the next morning.

Stillwater was besieged by media people and curiosity seekers. Two attractive eighteen year old women charged with two brutal, savage killings! There were headlines with pictures of Francine and Cindy. One picture showed Francine in her Girl Scout uniform. Girl Scout officials shuddered at the unwelcome publicity and were not surprised when membership declined on the local level in Stillwater. Neighbors of the slain couple and acquaintances of the girls were pestered unmercifully. Some took the phone off the hook and others left town for a few days to escape the nuisance.

Many people assumed a drug connection, and, despite police denials that drugs had been involved, there were some who could only explain the murders by saying, "They must have been high on drugs!"

There were others who suspected Satanism. A farmer who found some strange markings in his pasture called police to tell them that Satanists had been meeting there. (The police checked it out but were unable to find proof of devil worship. Some officers thought it was a prank.)

Fox Television produced a thirty minute program, *Current Affair*, on the Stepp murder case that was shown nationwide. The cameramen pictured the outside of the Stepp home, showing the spacious, comfortable home. The Stillwater High School, a one story brick building north of the main street was featured. The funeral home, with its glass cathedral type roof was pictured, and even the outside of the Payne County Jail, where the women were being held.

Current Affair reporters interviewed Francine's boyfriend on camera as he talked about the events. He said that Francine had wanted to move out of her parents' home to share an apartment with Cindy and that Francine's parents had not let her. He said that Francine felt her parents did not like her very much. There were two color photographs of Francine in happier days.

A neighbor of the Stepps was interviewed, and he stated that he had never known a friendlier or more crime-free neighborhood. A member of Mark and Dee's softball team remembered them as the camera panned the softball field and focused in on a photograph of the smiling couple. He mentioned that, even as he played ball now, he could feel Mark's presence and hear Dee's voice coming from the dugout. It was a moving moment.

A friend of both Cindy and Francine was shown on camera telling about her visit to them while they were in jail. She said Cindy's first words to her were, "I didn't do it!" But she added that Francine did not say anything to her. She thought Francine was terrified.

Classmates of Francine recalled that she was an average student and a member of the marching band, something of a loner, but they found it hard to believe that she could commit such a crime. Lieutenant Thrasher was shown in his office and spoke on camera, but he declined to comment on future developments.

It would appear that the case had been cleared by arrest and that the lawmen could relax and enjoy some deserved time off from the twelve and fourteen hour days they had put in during the intense investigation.

But, as the men sat around and talked about it, Bartram started worrying again.

"You know, it looks like we've got them dead to rights, but we've been out to the lake twice and still haven't found the gun," he confided to McGrath.

"That's because the girls can't agree on where they threw it. They can't even agree that they put in a bag. Francine says they did and Cindy says they just tossed it." McGrath shrugged.

"You know they did it, and I know they did it, but there are still a lot of loopholes in their stories that a good lawyer could drive a truck through," Bartram worried.

"What do you mean?"

"Well, the fingerprint, for instance. F. Lee Bailey would get up there and convince the jury that they were cooking hamburger meat the night before the murder and that's how Francine's fingerprint came to be on the glass."

"You're forgetting we've got their confessions on videotape. That's pretty hard to dispute."

"But a tricky lawyer could persuade a jury that the girls were brainwashed or that Francine was so traumatized by the sight of her parents' bodies that she just imagined she did it."

"Well, you can't get around the two witnesses hearing them plan it."

"Those two young men are pretty simpleminded. The likes of a Race Horse Haynes could twist them up so much by the time they finished testifying that the jury would disregard their testimony. Nope, I'm telling you we need to find that gun. If it turns up where they said they threw it, that would help our case a lot! And, I'd be real curious to see if there might be a second knife in the bag with the gun."

"Oh, you're referring to the autopsy report, where the good doctor says it's possible there were two knives, but she couldn't be sure?"

"Yes. It doesn't make sense to me that Dee Stepp, having been awakened by gunshots and seeing her husband lying there, would have waited in the bedroom for Francine to go to the kitchen and return with a knife and stab her to death, does it?"

"But if Francine had help from Cindy in stabbing them, why doesn't she say so?"

"I think the realization of the murders is too horrifying for Francine's conscience. Remember, this girl has been a Girl Scout and gone to Sunday School for years. I believe that she has blocked it out of her mind."

"Well, I think you worry too much. This case is wrapped up. We did a good job of investigation and now all we have to do is let the district attorney do his job and put these two away where they belong."

Chapter Four

There is a telephone "hot line" linking the Stillwater Police Department and Payne County Jail. On this day, July 14, the words came over the phone briskly, "We're bringing over two females charged with first degree murder."

The jailer taking the call responded in the affirmative and hung up the phone, turning to the deputy standing nearby. Rumors had been flying among the law enforcement officers working in the courthouse that the police were closing in on the perpetrators.

He repeated the message and the deputy nodded. All lawmen know, both from training and experience that one of the most crucial times in handling prisoners is the transfer from one facility to another. Simply being outside in the fresh air and sunshine may prove irresistibly tempting, goading a prisoner to make a desperate attempt at escape. Understanding this, the procedure for moving prisoners has been designed to prevent such lunges for freedom.

When the Payne County courthouse was remodeled and expanded, the jail was moved from the top floor (where one or two attempts at escape via knotted sheets led to fatal falls) to the basement, where it is now. There is a drive that goes under the parking lot, much like many hospitals have for their emergency rooms. The police car carrying the women from the municipal building, four blocks away, pulled up in front of the jail's double doors.

Smoothly, with ease of experience, the officers ushered the women in handcuffs to the receiving desk—a formica covered counter where they were asked questions to fill out the three forms required on each inmate. The police officers accompanying the women placed their weapons in the metal cabinet, locking each one individually and removing the keys. No one in the jail is allowed to carry guns, including the Sheriff's deputies, or the jailers themselves, beyond that point. The jailers are aware that even though the four to six trustees available to do the cooking, cleaning, and so on are usually reliable enough to help run the jail, they do not ever want to tempt an inmate, trustee or not, to make a try to grab for a gun.

The jailer on dayshift was Mark Hall, who has the muscular body of the weight lifter he was in college. He wears his uniform proudly, the spotless white shirt and brown pants pressed to perfection. His desire for neatness is revealed in the carefully quick movements as he puts everything in its proper place, from official forms, to the hand-washing liquid used before finger-printing. Hall had left for the day, so it was jailer Guy Posey, a twelve-year veteran who processed the women. Posey is a slender, brown haired man, clean shaven with a polite, courteous manner. Even potentially violent prisoners fail to ruffle his calm composure.

On the door of the room behind the receiving counter, is a huge poster in big black letters that spells out: *Guidelines for Obtaining Classifiable Fingerprints.*

1. Use black printer's ink.

2. Distribute ink evenly on inking slab.
3. Wash and dry fingers thoroughly.
4. Roll fingers from nail to nail and avoid allowing fingers to slip.
5. Be sure impressions are recorded in correct order.
6. If an amputation or deformity makes it impossible to print a finger, make a notation to that effect.
7. If some physical condition makes it impossible to print a finger, memos to that effect must be stapled to card to explain circumstances.

Below that list are three greatly enlarged examples of loops, whorls, and arches with arrows pointing to the lines running between deltas that must be clear, with the notation that arches have no deltas.

Swiftly, Posey showed first Francine and then Cindy how to press each finger to the electrically controlled inking machine and then helped them roll each finger to obtain a clear print. Then each woman was requested to stand against the white painted wall with height designations painted on it. A camera swings out from the wall on a bracket. Francine appeared totally emotionless as she held the date placard in front of her chest. Even the usually irrepressible Cindy seemed subdued by the procedure. They may have been drained by the emotional confession scenes played out at the police station, or perhaps they were beginning to realize they were actually going to be confined in jail.

Posey was told by the accompanying officers that the women had already been searched by a female officer of the Stillwater Police Department. Ruth Stites, deputy and office manager of the Payne County jail is a fiftyish woman of medium build with lots of dark curly hair, brown eyes and a friendly smile. She normally searches the women that are booked into the jail. When she is not available, the jailers request a woman from the Stillwater Police Department or failing to find a woman on duty there, they request a female officer from the OSU security force. No man is ever allowed to lay his hands on any woman in the Payne County jail and there has been no scandal in Payne County, unlike some other counties in the state.

Ruth Stites escorted them to their cells and informed them of the rules. This information is also prominently displayed upstairs in the office where visitors sign in. The rules for long term prisoners are:

1. One change of clothing (laundry is done on premises)
2. Writing paper, stamps, one pencil and envelopes
3. Limited amount of money for cigarettes and candy
4. Toothpaste and toothbrush
5. Shampoo and deodorants in plastic containers only.
6. One paperback book
7. Medication by prescription only. This will be dispensed by jailer on duty, as needed.

Attorneys, Ministers, Counselors, Case Workers, etc. may visit whenever necessary. All others are strictly limited to regular visiting hours.

Ruth told them they could have a TV set in their cells, if their families wanted to provide them with one. Then she showed them to the 9' x 12' cell they would call home until their trials.

All the basement cells and halls are painted white ceilings and white walls to forty inches off the floor, which is painted navy blue. This two-toned color scheme was favored by the preceding Sheriff, Frank Phillips, and the current Sheriff, Carl Hiner, has seen no need to change it.

The steep steps leading down from the upstairs office are painted red and large signs read: Caution, Watch Your Step. These cautionary signs are primarily for the benefit of the visitors.

There are accommodations for up to eight women, with two- tiered bunks on each side, but the usual occupation is two or three. During the record breaking drought of 1988, the cells held four young women. Francine and Cindy were placed in separate cells.

Both Mark Hall and Ruth Stites state the women were never any problem, although they recall that sometimes Cindy and Francine would get mad at each other, with Cindy screaming at Francine, "I hate you! I hate you! I hate you for getting me into this!"

Francine would usually respond by retreating to the farthest corner of her cell and sitting with her arms locked around her knees, occasionally looking over towards Cindy's cell with venom in her eyes.

Jailers are strict in enforcing the No Graffiti on the walls rules, and when the inevitable writing appears, the inmates are obliged to scrub it off. Above the bars, on the inside of the cell, where the jailers cannot observe it, both Cindy and Francine managed to write their names many times. Except for court appearances, makeup is not allowed, and this is bitterly complained about.

Francine shared her cell with a Native American woman, younger than herself, who was implicated in a robbery. They played cards, watched TV together, and simply waited out the passage of time together, but they never became good friends. Francine's roommate was to confide in her boyfriend that she was afraid of Francine.

"Francine killed them. I know that. She said she'd kill me too, if I ever said she told me she done it."

Cindy's and Francine's moods would vary. Sometimes they were elaborately polite and at other times, for no apparent reason, they were filled with rage. Especially when Cindy returned from meetings with her attorney, she seemed particularly upset and would alternate between vilifying Francine and shrieking, "I hate you!" to her.

Francine seemed to be numb a lot of the time. After her attorney sessions, her cellmate said Francine seemed depressed and unusually quiet, and she was never very talkative. The jailers said she always seemed acquiescent to their requests, never giving them any back talk or trouble. Occasionally she would request another paperback book to read.

The visiting room is a small room with four cubicles, and stools on each side of the dividing wall, reminiscent of a 1950s lunch counter. Beside the four small glass windows are four phones for the parties to communicate with each other. It is daunting for anyone unfamiliar with jails to undergo the routine of signing in and being shown to the room behind locked doors, so it is no wonder Francine and Cindy were not overwhelmed with visits from friends. Francine's boyfriend had just been released from a driving under the influence charge, so was ineligible to visit her. They corresponded and Francine wrote that she would be out in a month or two. He was not told that she had confessed to the murder, so he believed her and told her that he would wait for her.

The only visitors permitted back inside the cells who have actual physical contact with the prisoners are the ministers and the minister's wives. At Francine's request, her beauty operator, Debbie House, was allowed to cut her hair before her court appearance.

Debbie repeated her belief in Francine's innocence to everyone who came into the beauty shop. She kept repeating, "I know that she didn't do it. Dee loved Francine and Francine loved her mother. I just know she didn't do it!"

Ruth met Francine's aunts and thought they were lovely ladies. She found herself becoming fond of Francine and Cindy. Francine asked her opinion on the clothing she wore to court—a short sleeved pale blue blouse and straight navy skirt.

"Do you think the skirt's too long?"

Ruth responded, "I think you look very nice." Privately, she thought Francine's attorney had stressed that they should look ladylike and not try to appear "punk" and she agreed that a conservative look was best.

The most frequent visitors Francine and Cindy had were Jeannie Stafford, no relation, a Baptist minister's wife and Deanne Ketch, from the same church.

These are the type of dedicated women who respond when needed, whether it is to comfort a young couple on the death of a baby or to help a family worn out at the deathbed vigil of an aging parent. Both Jeannie and Deanne were primarily interested in helping the women find peace of heart and mind. They were elated that at one of the church services conducted at the jail the women "answered the call".

"Francine and Cindy have found the Lord now. They are praying with us and reading their Bibles and they are saved!"

The jailer who heard this did not argue with them, but he recalled with cynicism how many inmates suddenly "found the Lord" when they heard the cell doors slam shut behind them, and how quickly they lost religion when they were released.

One day, after Francine requested another pair of shoes, the visitor arrived with a pair of shoes at the reception counter and Mark Hall searched them carefully, finding nothing secreted in them.

"Okay, you can take them back to her." Hall walked with the visitor back to Francine's cell and was standing to observe that nothing else but the shoes changed hands, when he suddenly heard the sound of an indrawn breath. Both he and the visitor stared at Francine, who had gone white. Stammering, she said, "Those aren't *my* shoes."

Instantly they realized whose shoes they were. Embarrassed, the visitor quickly reassured Francine that she would return with another pair.

Oddly, it was not long after that incident that Francine requested the picture of her parents and herself that had appeared in the *Daily O'Collegian* newspaper, be brought to her. She wanted to keep it in her cell. That request was denied.

Neither of the minister's wives who were regular visitors ever talked about the crime with Francine or Cindy. Their sole concerns were with their spiritual lives, and that the authorities were treating the women right. Both women felt Francine's conversion sincere, and while they were willing to give Cindy the benefit of the doubt, the women admitted that they weren't so sure about Cindy's newfound love of God.

Chapter Five

District Attorney Paul Anderson is a big Teddy-bear of a man, ruggedly good looking with curly brownish grey hair, bald on top, and a quiet, friendly demeanor. He has four assistants, but to cover the duties of prosecuting attorney for both Payne and Logan counties, he still works sixty hour weeks. He arrives in his office by seven-thirty a.m. and leaves around six p.m. or later.

The District Attorney's offices were redecorated in the spring of 1988. Now there is a tasteful glass door with the crest of the office on it that opens to the receptionist's desk. Down a long, grey carpeted hall, past the assistant's offices and three secretaries desks, at the end of the hall is Anderson's office, with a huge walnut desk, soft padded couch and two arm chairs. Books line the wall behind the desk and a brass coat rack stands in the corner.

Before remodeling, the door stood open most of the time to the vestibule where two secretaries worked, court reporters shared offices with assistants, chairs were lined up against the wall, and it was a noisy and confusing place. Everyone involved agrees that there is now better utilization of work space.

Anderson says, "The District Attorney for a metropolitan area has an easier time, in one way, in that not everyone of his constituents expects to speak with the District Attorney himself." Payne and Logan county residents, from a heavily rural background, expect to speak with the District Attorney if it's a case of a vandalized mail box, stolen pig, or missing lawn furniture. Being an elected official, he tries to oblige.

The previous District Attorney, James Langley, was killed, along with his assistant, in a private plane crash in 1982. They were flying low over the Cimarron River, looking for evidence of a field of marijuana and crashed into the sandy river bank. Anderson was appointed to fill out the term. He stood for reelection in 1986 and was unopposed.

Lawton, Oklahoma, where Anderson was born sits on the south edge of the state and is home to Fort Sill Army base. Thousands of soldiers have trained there, from the earliest cavalry days of the Indian wars, to the armored units of today. Western frontier heritage is strong in the town, with the oldest residents still able to recall the last uprising of Crazy Snake and the days when open saloons and brothels were common. The small town of Geronimo, named for the famous Apache Chief, is located just south of Lawton.

Today the H. E. Bailey turnpike angles south from Oklahoma City through Lawton to Wichita Falls, Texas. Motels line the turnpike as well as the older Highway 62 that runs north and south through town. The business sections of Lawton appear prosperous due in part to the money circulated from the army base.

Anderson is the older of two children. His favorite class in grade school was English. He liked sports and was an eager player on grade school teams. His father was a comptroller for civil service at Fort Sill and after twenty years there he retired to serve ten years on the Lawton City Council. Anderson's mother worked part time at the Savings and Loan company as a closer on real estate transactions.

Anderson remembers his grandparents fondly. His grandfather, Paul W. Anderson was an oil field worker for Gulf Oil. As a boy he used to visit his grandparents home in Seminole, Oklahoma. At that time oil field workers were provided houses that were called "shotgun" houses. Rows of identical frame buildings edged the oil refinery and the houses were built with a screened-in front porch, living room, kitchen and bedrooms, all in a narrow rectangular configuration. Someone once said you could stand at the front door and hit everyone inside with a shotgun, hence the term.

While the Andersons were not poor while Paul was growing up, their living conditions were modest and he was exposed to the value of hard work and a conservative attitude towards money. He was active in sports and today enjoys quail hunting, bass fishing (he does not own a boat) and playing tennis. There was no particular role models to inspire him to enter the study of law, except for one uncle who was an attorney, but after graduation from Lawton High School, he enrolled at Oklahoma University in Norman, successfully graduating from the University and the Law School there and passing the bar exam. He married his wife, Linda, in 1966. She is a registered physical therapist with her own private practice. They have two sons, teenagers, Luke and Seth.

Anderson served in the Judge Advocates office in Colorado Springs from 1969 to 1972. Then he moved to

Stillwater, where he served as assistant District Attorney until he decided to open his own private practice, which he operated until the fatal accident in 1982, when he was appointed to finish out the term of the late James Langley.

Anderson, by the nature of his job, sees many autopsy reports, diagrams of bodies and photographs taken at the scene of crimes. Through the years he has grown able to view these items with detachment, but the violence of the Stepp murders was shocking to him. It surprised him when day after day the accused women were able to maintain an icy calm when details of the murders were discussed in the courtroom. There were times when he felt more shaken than they appeared. Both young women, he felt, were pretty good actresses, in the way in which they controlled their emotions.

On July 14, both Francine Stepp and Cindy Wynn signed applications for appointed attorneys. The application form has fifteen questions on it, asking such things as name, age, marital status, dependents, how are you supported? If you receive welfare, give details. If employed, how much money do you make? To the question, how much money do you have at the present time? Cindy Wynn wrote $6.77. To the same questions, Francine Stepp answered $50 and $550 in the bank. To the question, do you own a car, real estate, life insurance, stocks, bonds, hobby equipment, collections, jewelry, etc? Cindy wrote zero and Francine answered that she owned items worth approximately $500.

Cheryl Ramsey was appointed to defend Cindy Wynn and Jack Bowyer was appointed to defend Francine Stepp. Ms. Ramsey is a trim blonde, attractive and businesslike. Bowyer is dark haired, stocky built, shorter than Anderson. Bowyer lives in Perkins, a small town ten miles south of

Stillwater. In Oklahoma, the maximum amount a court appointed attorney can receive for defending a murder defendant is $3,200. There were two murder charges, so the defense attorneys were entitled to $6,400 each. They could also recover some items of expense incurred in preparing the case.

The first thing the newly appointed defense attorneys did was to request permission to visit the scene of the crime. They then filed motions to quash and suppress the arrests and charges filed against the defendants. Ms. Ramsey, on Wynn's behalf, requested that necessary expenses for expert polygraph examiner, private investigator and other independent experts be allowed. She was told the request was premature.

The two defense attorneys requested the addresses of all the witnesses be provided. They also made a motion for criminal records of all witnesses be disclosed. They requested a motion to secure copies of all newspaper articles and video tapes and audio tapes at the State's expense. They requested material from Tulsa television Channels 2, 6 and 8, and Oklahoma City Channels 4, 5 and 9, filing a subpoena with the court for out-of-county material.

July 20, 1988 was the date set for the first preliminary hearing. The purpose of the hearing was to determine if a crime had been committed and secondly if there was probable cause to believe either or both of the defendants committed the crime.

Ms. Ramsey asked that the defendants' statements be given the defense attorneys and asked the court to recess to allow them to view police reports, confessions, any items that come into evidence. She said, "I want to put the Court on notice that I'm not going to take a quick look at something and go into cross examination." She cited past court cases favoring early disclosure, as soon as practical following the filing of charges. Bowyer concurred with her lengthy statements and asked for material, even if it was premature to do so.

Anderson said at that point, "Their arguments to the Court are pretty novel, but they are candid. It's like, Your Honor, the Court of Criminal Appeals doesn't provide for it, there is no case law, but we would like to go ahead and violate the law and ask the prosecution to dump over their files."

Ramsey and Bowyer both protested.

Judge Belden agreed with Anderson, and repeated, "The purpose of this hearing is to determine *if* a crime has been committed, and secondly, if there is probable cause to believe either or both of defendants committed this crime."

After reviewing the evidence presented, the Court denied a motion to set bond, and after further motions were noted by the court, the defendants were remanded to custody of the Payne County Jailer. The date of the next hearing was set for September 5th.

Chapter Six

The Payne County courthouse stands in the center of a tree-shaded block just one block from Stillwater's Main Street. Across from it to the north is the Public Library, on the west is Bernhardt's Strode Funeral Home, to the south is the First Baptist Church and office buildings and to the east is the Stillwater Savings and Loan building and the Greiner buildings, with a restaurant upstairs and jewelry store downstairs.

The courthouse grounds are the site of the Run For the Arts, arts and crafts festival each year, the Veterans programs on Memorial and Armistice days and the scene of political speeches. With the advent of television, not as much political activity happens outdoors as in earlier times, when it was not unusual for free food and drinks to be served after the marathon political speech-making.

The first courthouse was a two-story wood frame building built in 1892, when Oklahoma was still Indian Territory. It had stairs on the outside leading up to the second floor. The reason for the outside stairway was a matter of economy. In case of a hanging, they could use the second story landing as part of the gallows.

The court clerk wrote in long hand, in the evenings by light of kerosene lamps. Community meetings were held in the courthouse, and once when four men were carrying a piano up the flight of stairs, a man's grasp on the piano slipped and the instrument plunged to the ground. Incredibly, it did not suffer much damage, and was used at the community meetings held in the courthouse.

From the pictures collected by Robert Cunningham, Stillwater historian, it is evident that the first building was built off the ground with space underneath it. Small animals, dogs and an occasional skunk wandered in. The building burned in 1894, and was replaced with another wooden building in 1895, built at a cost of $595.

At that time court sessions lasted a month and covered everything from motions and demurrers, default divorce and default cases, then the criminal cases were heard, followed by civil jury cases. The windows of the courtroom were left open to let breezes come in, along with flies, mosquitos and an occasional wasp or bee.

The first judge, John H. Burford, according to his chronicler, Thomas A Higgins, court clerk, was a stickler for correct dress. The Judge habitually wore high collars, tie and long black silk coat, no matter how hot the weather.

He was a popular and respected judge, both by the early settlers and the members of the bar. The next judge came from Guthrie and his judicial district covered six counties.

The early day judges were more concerned with dispensing justice than in the finer points of law. Judge A. H. Huston often said, "My chief concern is to determine which side is right. Once I've determined that I can always muster a reason for my decision."

Very few appeals were taken from either of the first two judges, the pioneers evidently feeling they had been dealt with fairly.

As statehood was granted in 1907, the Payne County Courthouse became an even busier place. It was painted slate grey by this time, but in 1917 the excavation was begun and the cornerstone of the present day courthouse was laid. Lumber from the old courthouse was used by residents in construction of private homes and buildings.

Compared to the two previous buildings, the new building was palatial. Marble and brick, with Ionic columns and a central steam heating system. The jail was on the top floor. Construction was delayed by World War I, so that the open house for the new building wasn't held until January 25, 1919.

The first law enforcement officers for Payne County were United States Deputy Marshalls, Christ Madsen, Bill Tilghman and Heck Thomas. All are mentioned and some of them idolized in western movies. The early residents of Stillwater depended on the Marshalls, along with a City Marshall and a night watchman. It wasn't until the 1920s that Stillwater formed an official police department with a police chief and a two man force.

In 1968 the Payne County Courthouse was remodeled by adding on to the west side of the building, space was nearly doubled and the jail was moved to the basement. While the builders tried to match the red brick of the original building, it is evident from the modern appearance of the windows which part has been added on. Meanwhile the Stillwater Police Department was growing. From the tiny nucleus in the early days, it grew to an eight man force. A police car was added in 1936. Before the days of mobile phones, a flashing red light at the corner of Main Street and Ninth Street alerted the officer on patrol to call the police dispatcher. In 1939 the police department moved to the new City Hall building at 723 South Lewis. Each year the Policeman's Ball raised money to outfit the department. Improvements followed rapidly, a darkroom and complete photography section was instituted by Glen Shirley. Radio communication came into the police department the same year World War II started. The department now had seventeen members. By 1968 the force had grown to thirty and a Teletype machine was added as well as a mobile radar unit. Cooperation between Stillwater Police Department and Payne County Sheriff has always been good. There are only a half dozen Sheriff Deputies to cover an area forty miles wide by twenty miles long, much of it rural.

In 1987, private funds were donated to redecorate the district courtroom. The courtroom is a circular room at the end of the third floor. The marble steps leading up to the third floor separate the two hallways to the chamber at the end. The elevator is west of the stairs in the part added in 1968. Entering the courtroom, you see the marble divider that separates the spectators from the officials and the participants. Counsels and their parties sit behind walnut grained tables in front of the judge's bench, behind which is the great seal of Oklahoma and a US flag on one side with an Oklahoma flag on the other. The court reporter sits at an angle to the bench and the jury sits in seats on the east side of the courtroom, the back row of seats higher than the front row to facilitate viewing.

The carpet is a deep royal blue and the white sheer curtains covering the venetian blinds at the windows are topped by navy blue swags. The Grecian design of the front pillars are repeated in the marble window frames. It is an impressive room and it is instinctive for spectators to lower their voices and talk in a hush, even when the room is empty.

The courtroom was far from empty the days Francine Stepp and Cindy Wynn were brought in for their initial preliminary hearings. People arrived early to get a seat. Besides interested friends and relatives, reporters from local newspapers and the Channel 4 television news people were there.

In contrast to the portraits of Territorial Judges, Judge Lois Belden is a woman of medium height and build, with short, blonde hair. She wore glasses and outside the courtroom had a pleasant smile and demeanor. Presiding over preliminary hearings, she presented a more solemn, serious appearance.

The purpose of the hearings were to determine if there was sufficient evidence to bind the defendants over for trial. Some states have a grand jury system to do this in confidentiality. Oklahoma has a grand jury system, mostly used when there is suspicion of wrong doing by judicial, legislative or law enforcement officials. The hearings for Francine Stepp and Cindy Wynn were open, public hearings, at which time the defense attorneys and the district attorney prosecuting the case, would go over the material presented and most importantly size each other up. Each side was looking for weakness or points that could be used to each one's benefit.

The court appointed attorneys, Cheryl Ramsey for Cindy Wynn and Jack Bowyer for Francine Stepp responded affirmatively when the Judge asked if they were prepared. District Attorney Paul Anderson was eager to get on with it.

The first hour and a half were taken up with legal maneuverings and motions, all duly noted and addressed. The spectators were quietly bored and some yawned at the incomprehensible legal terms. They were curious and anxious for the proceedings to get interesting.

The first witness to the stand was Jim Posey, best friend and neighbor to Mark Stepp.

When asked by the district attorney, he gave his full name, address and place of employment.

"For what period of time were you acquainted with Mark and Delores Stepp?"

He answered, "I had known Mark for approximately twenty-six years and had known Delores for about eighteen years."

"Did you know them before you moved to Stillwater?"

"Yes."

"And where did that acquaintance begin?"

"As I said, I had known Mark for about twenty-six years, knew him in high school, we were friends in high school and we had both been members of..."

Bowyer, Francine's attorney, objected that it was not responsive to the question asked. The Judge sustained it.

The District Attorney continued his questioning, "What town did your acquaintance begin?"

"Fon Du Lac, Wisconsin."

"My question to you, sir, did you ever have occasion to sell or give a firearm to either Delores or Mark Stepp?"

"Yes, I did."

It was brought out that Posey had sold a Ruger .22 caliber automatic, with six inch tapered barrel, to his friend and neighbor for seventy five dollars. The firearm was housed in a wooden, felt-lined case. Posey had no idea where in the house Mark Stepp kept his gun.

Then the DA Anderson asked, "For what purpose did Mr. Stepp require the firearm?"

Bowyer objected and the court sustained the objection, so the district attorney went on to other things.

"Have you seen the firearm subsequent to the time you sold it to Mark Stepp?"

"Not to the best of my recollection, no."

"Do you know where he kept it?"

Ms. Ramsey objected at that point, since the witness said he hadn't seen it since he sold the gun.

Both attorneys for the defense questioned him without adding anything material to the case.

Then Doctor Chai S. Choi was called to the stand.

The district attorney asked her occupation.

Doctor Choi, slender and professional-looking in a dark suit with white blouse, answered, "Currently I am forensic pathologist working with the Office of Chief Medical Examiner in Oklahoma City for the State of Oklahoma."

"How long have you been employed in that capacity?"

"Since March, 1983, sir."

"And prior to that time where were you employed?"

"I was in the residency program at the Chief Medical Examiner's office in Salt Lake City of the State of Utah."

"And would you briefly describe your education for the Court, your degrees?"

"Yes, sir. First of all, I graduated from the School of Medicine in Seoul, Korea, and came to the United States and received a four year residency in anatomical pathology and a two year residency in clinical pathology and a two year residency in forensic pathology at the Chief Medical Examiner's Office in Salt Lake City, Utah. And immediately I obtained medical board certification of both anatomical, clinical and forensic pathology and joined the current office, Chief Medical Examiner in Oklahoma City as a forensic pathologist."

"During the course of your employment with the State Medical Examiner's office, have you had occasion to perform autopsies and if so, how many?"

She answered, "Yes, sir. Overall, close to a thousand cases, sir."

"What is the purpose of an autopsy? Why is an autopsy performed?"

"For the determination of a cause of death and providing the manner of death of the decedent."

"And with that explanation, did you have an occasion to perform an autopsy on the bodies of Delores and Mark Stepp?"

"Yes, sir, I did."

The autopsies were performed at the morgue, 901 North Stonewall, Oklahoma City, on June 9, 1988 in the afternoon about 1:50 p.m. with assistant pathologist Joel Grog and Officer Graham present.

Asked to describe the wounds on the body of Delores Stepp, the courtroom became still as death. There were no sounds of people shifting in their seats or clearing their throats, as there had been earlier during the legal discussions. The spectators knew only the newspaper accounts of "multiple stab wounds". This would be the first time they would hear the full extent of the injuries.

"Overall, there were multiple stab wounds to her chest and back and one knife was stuck into her back and several scratches, bruises and some cuts."

"Any other wounds?"

"That's all, other than just recent bruises to the legs."

Asked to be more specific, she replied, "One was in the

right knee. The other bruise was on the left thigh that showed to be at least a twenty-four-hour old bruise."

"What was the cause of death for Delores Stepp?"

"Multiple stab wounds."

At this point several diagrams were introduced, labeled and marked for identification purposes as State's Exhibits. To confirm that no evidence had been tampered with, the district attorney then asked how the knife was removed from Delores Stepp's body.

Doctor Choi replied that she had used a hemostat, a little metallic clamp and then handed it to one of the agents, Mr. Nick Graham who then packaged it.

They moved on to the autopsy of Mark Stepp.

"Would you describe the physical damage to the body?"

"Yes, sir. There were multiple stab wounds to his chest and right forearm and some cuts, and a gunshot injury wound on his right chest."

"Could you point out to the court and to the defendants the location on the body? I can see it here in medical terms, but so we can understand it, could you point to yourself where the bullet entered?"

She pointed to herself and said, "This bullet appeared to pass under the skin and came out at the base of the neck on the right, where I'm pointing again, and then re-entered into the body and that bullet hit the backbone, which is the thoracic spine number one and two, which I might point at, using my back around here."

While Doctor Choi was speaking, Francine kept her head down, with her gaze fastened on the floor in front of her. Cindy sighed occasionally and appeared bored with the proceedings. She shifted in her chair so that the spectators could see her profile, and rolled her eyes upward in an exaggerated expression of disgust.

Again, the district attorney wanted to make it clear the evidence had been carefully preserved, so he asked, "Did you remove the projectile?"

Upon her affirmative response, he asked, "And to whom did you deliver the projectile?"

"In my presence, I delivered it to one of the agents named Nick Graham and he held it for me. I wrote on it for identification."

"Was the projectile intact or was it fragmented and if so, how many pieces?"

"I recovered one deformed lead bullet, which is sizewise about small."

"Based on the location of the bullet and the examination of the method of entry, did you draw any conclusions about the particular damage to the body that it caused that is noted in your reports?"

"Yes, sir. Based upon the wound which hit the spinal cord, which immediately paralyzed his body below the T-1, which is thoracic number one, which is his legs and arms were not able to move."

"So if I understand you, you are saying when he was struck by this bullet, it is your medical opinion that he became paralyzed and was unable to move?"

"That's right, sir."

"Would he have been able to defend himself?"

Bowyer objected that the question called for a speculation of the witness. He stated that there had been no testimony on whether Mr. Stepp was stabbed first or shot first.

Anderson responded, "I think that's a conclusion that she can draw, your honor."

Judge Belden agreed to allow the question, since it was relevant. She told Bowyer, "Your exception is noted."

Turning back to Doctor Choi, Anderson asked, "Based upon your statement and the likelihood of paralysis, would the victim Stepp have been able to defend himself?"

"In my opinion, probably not."

Then she was asked if Mark Stepp's body bore any defensive wounds.

"The stab on the right forearm could have been the defense wound, but that is a possibility."

Asked to explain her conclusions, Doctor Choi continued, "It usually depends on the injury. The favorite sites are arms, which is naturally where they try to defend and cover up the important area of the body. And the second one, against that, that this man, I don't know if the shot was first or last before the stabbing wound on the right forearm for two reasons. That's why the stab wound of the right forearm could have been a defense wound."

"In your examination, did you conclude that the arm could have been placed here? Did any wound in the chest correspond with the through and through wound in the arm?"

"It is possible, but not likely, sir."

"With respect to your autopsy of Delores Stepp, did your examination of those wounds reveal any wounds which you had determined to be defensive wounds or wounds she incurred while defending herself against attack?"

"Yes, there are several wounds suggesting those were wounds that could have been defense wounds, which are those injuries located on both forearms and hands. Several bruises and cuts shown in both arms and hands."

"Based on your examination in your autopsy, what was the cause of death of Delores Stepp?"

"Multiple stab wounds."

Then Anderson offered State's Exhibits that were original diagrams of the body into evidence. They are part of the official report that is required to be filed with the state. The diagrams for Mark Stepp's body were then admitted without objection.

The knife was introduced into evidence, with accompanying statements as to the time and witnesses that observed it being sealed for evidence.

Following that, the district attorney sat down, and Jack Bowyer commenced to question Doctor Choi.

He started off by asking her to pronounce her last name, which she did. Then he asked, "Dr. Choi, did you rely on any information supplied to you through written means to form an opinion in this case? Let me rephrase that. The opinion that you formed pertaining to the cause of death, was that arrived at before you viewed the bodies or after you conducted an in-depth autopsy?"

"After a complete conduction of the autopsy."

"Now, at approximately what time did you start conducting the first autopsy?"

"Delores Stepp was about eight-thirty in the morning."

Bowyer then asked if the body had been at the facility all night and when she said that it had, he asked her to describe the storage facility. She answered that the bodies were stored in refrigeration about four degrees centigrade.

Bowyer inquired if Dr. Choi used a manual pertaining to the autopsy. She replied that she had a routine manual that contains the original of the admission of the body and a brief report about the information surrounding the person's death. The manual lists any evidence or material obtained from the body which is submitted before performing autopsy and it, as well as the body is photographed. Then the external body surfaces are inspected for injuries or disease. Then the internal organs are examined for the confirmation or determination of the cause of death.

Bowyer asked about the bruises on Delores Stepps' legs and Dr. Choi could not be more precise than she had been about the time of the bruising, although she had measured the bruises to the centimeter.

Then the defense attorney and the Korean doctor began sparring over a form that had been included in the report.

"Do you check all individuals you do autopsies on for hepatitis?"

"No, sir, it is not routine procedure."

"Was it conducted on Mark Stepp and Delores Stepp?"

When she replied in the negative, Bowyer requested that she turn to a certain page in the report, so that he could ask questions about it.

Dr. Choi pointed out that the page in question did not concern a hepatitis test. Still doubting that she was correct, Bowyer demanded, "What type of test is it?"

"This is Acquired Immune Deficiency Syndrome."

"Excuse me?"

"Acquired Immune Deficiency Syndrome, what is called AIDS."

Some of the spectators muffled a snicker. If Bowyer had thought to shake up the state's witness, he had failed to do so and managed to make himself look less than knowledgeable.

"Okay, that's what this report is?"

"Yes."

"And what were those results?"

"All turned out to be negative."

They discussed the bruises on her arms and legs some more. Then Bowyer asked about the size and shape of the instrument used to make the stab wounds.

"Now, comparisons of the wounds between Mark Stepp and Delores Stepp as far as penetrating wounds, can you say with medical certainty that Mark Stepp and Delores Stepp were stabbed with the same item or instrument?"

"Could have been."

They went back over the size and similarities of the wounds, but Doctor Choi would never say with certainty that they were all committed with the same knife, only that they might have been. Several spectators looked at each other with upraised eyebrows. There might be another knife used in murder out there somewhere!

Then Bowyer went on to the gunshot wound. He asked, "Did you form a medical opinion on the angle that the projectile had come from?"

"I only determined the direction of the gunshot in his body."

"Okay. What was the direction of the gunshot in his body?"

Doctor Choi explained that though it appeared externally that the bullet traveled upwards toward the medial backward, internal examination showed a somewhat different angle, traveling downward.

Bowyer asked for clarification and Doctor Choi said it appeared that the arms were raised at the time of being shot. When asked if she knew if Mark Stepp was right handed or left handed, she answered she did not know.

"Did you conduct any sort of medical examination as far as a paraffin test or such in regard to either one of Mr. Stepp's hands, his right or his left?"

"No, sir."

"Did you conduct any sort of an examination to determine whether there was powder residue?"

"Yes. I looked for powder residue around the wounds in his body surface, but there was no powder residue."

Bowyer asked if some object, such as a pillow, would have been placed between the gun and Mr. Stepp, would there have been a powder residue? Dr. Choi replied that it would be a matter of speculation, but it could be.

Once again, Bowyer asked at what point Mark Stepp was paralyzed and Doctor Choi answered that he was paralyzed promptly after being shot.

They discussed the diagrams drawn of Mark Stepp's body and the diagrams of Delores Stepp's body. Bowyer asked, "Your diagrams of the instrument responsible are different, correct?"

"Yes, sizewise they are a little different."

He went on to ask about the bullet, and the particular witnesses and way in which the bullet was sealed and submitted to the Stillwater Police department. After satisfying himself of those details, Bowyer moved on to ask what other type of items were removed from Delores Stepp's body?

"Fingernails from each hand."

Since there were no more questions about the fingernails, evidently there had been no skin particles found under them. Bowyer asked if Dr. Choi had conducted any tests to determine if Delores Stepp had been sexually assaulted. Dr. Choi referred to her notes and replied that she had obtained samples from the victim's mouth, anal and vaginal canals through swabbing. There was no indication that a sexual assault had occurred, since there was no injury to the vagina. In conducting the autopsy she learned that Delores Stepp had had a tubal ligation, to prevent pregnancy. There were no tumors in the body, she was a healthy woman of five feet four inches and sixty eight kilograms, roughly one hundred fifty pounds.

Bowyer inquired as to the exact stomach contents, and Dr. Choi replied that it looked hot dog meat type materials. The blood alcohol level report was missing from her file, and was never located. It is routine procedure to include this information and Dr. Choi was visibly upset that she was unable to locate it.

He asked if any foreign substance was contained within the stab wounds on Mark Stepp's body and was told there was none. Concerning the stab wounds on Mark Stepp's body the information was elicited that the deepest wound was 13.5 centimeters.

She was asked if the decedents were relatively healthy individuals and she replied that they were.

"From reviewing your reports, Doctor, and conducting this autopsy on Mark and Delores Stepp, you cannot say who did this, can you?"

"No, sir."

Bowyer concluded his cross-examination and it was time for Cheryl Ramsey, Cindy Wynn's attorney, to ask questions.

Ms. Ramsey's blonde hair was styled fashionably. She wore a tailored navy blue suit with white lace-trimmed blouse and black high heeled pumps.

"Doctor Choi, could you tell anything about the individual or individuals that were involved in the stabbings by looking at the wounds as far as their height, weight, right hand, left hand, etcetera?"

At first the doctor thought she meant the bodies for autopsy, but when she realized she was being asked about the assailants, she answered, "No. I don't know. I have never done that."

"All right. Now, I did not understand your answer to Mr. Bowyer's questions with regard to the bruises on the legs. Did those occur at the same time as the stabbings?"

"What I said was around the same time, just immediately before, just after or during."

"All right. Does the refrigeration of the bodies affect in any way the bruising? Does that stop the bruising from continuing through its normal course, if Mrs. Stepp had been alive?"

"Not at all."

"It goes ahead and goes through the normal process?"

"Right. Other than decaying."

Then the questioning proceeded to the subject of the toxicology reports and missing blood alcohol test on Delores Stepp's body. Ms. Ramsey asked if there was anything else missing from the report and was told that everything was included, with the exception of some photographs taken of the bodies and retained by the doctor.

At that point Ms. Ramsey requested that she be allowed to see the photographs. The Judge suggested a short recess while the photographs were being collected, but the District Attorney said, "There are not that many. We have got other people stacked up down there."

Judge Belden said, "All right, very good."

Dr. Choi testified that the brown manila envelope held three Polaroid pictures and sixty-four Kodachrome slides for both Mark and Delores Stepp. The slides were taken at the morgue and the Polaroid pictures were taken at the scene. After being informed that she would be required to sign a Court Order for the copies of the pictures to be released to the defense counsels, she was allowed to step down and return to Oklahoma City.

Unnatural Death is the title of a book by Michael M. Baden, New York Medical Examiner, with Judith Adler Hennessee.

In the book, Doctor Baden makes several salient points: medical examiners frequently see things no one else sees, the deaths that need not have happened, the failures of society. Medical examiners are different than hospital pathologists who autopsy bodies to study for disease. Forensic pathology is an untaught specialty, according to Dr. Baden. After medical school it is only by serving an apprenticeship that the medical examiner becomes an expert at determining and analyzing traumatic injuries.

Dr. Baden has had a long and illustrious career and has determined the cause of death from the evidence of tens of thousands of victims. He relates a little of the history of Oklahoma's method of death investigation.

In the 1960s in Oklahoma City, a prominent citizen's son by the name of George Cole was indicted for murder. It seems he and two college friends got into a brawl with a twenty-four-year-old man who died after a fight with Cole. A hospital pathologist who did the autopsy diagnosed death from a brain hemorrhage caused by a punch received in the fight, which made it a homicide.

At the trial it was shown that the pathologist misinterpreted his findings. Evidence was brought out that the victim had been suffering from a headache, was disoriented, acting peculiarly and that he started the fight. When he fell down, it was because of the aneurysm, not the fight. He died of natural causes, and the accused was acquitted of murder.

The case made headlines and shortly after that the state of Oklahoma established a Medical Examiner's office headed by a forensic pathologist. There was just one big problem, the state of Oklahoma shied away from funding it. Forced to use a local hospital's facilities, which rather naturally infuriated the hospital's staff, the state Medical Examiner autopsied a body in the field outside the hospital. He made his point, and shortly afterward, the office received the necessary funding.

Still, for sheer numbers the office in Oklahoma sees nothing like the number of bodies that are examined in the state of New York. It would have been interesting to learn if Doctor Baden could have determined whether the killer was right or left handed or if one or two knives were used.

The entry wound is measured very exactly at autopsy and a cross section of each wound is measured. The silicone in Delores Stepp's breasts and the muscular composition of the male body as contrasted with the female's body was the reason Dr. Choi gave for being uncertain on these points. The charts illustrating the wounds were introduced as state exhibits 44, 45, 46 and 47.

The court was recessed until the following day. A little crowd of court-watchers, devoted spectators who had been present during all the testimony gathered at a sandwich shop with the unlikely name, (in Oklahoma) of New York Bagel shop.

September 8th dawned bright and clear. It was a hot day, but not as bad as the scorching summer days had been. The crowd outside the district courtroom shuffled around impatiently waiting for the doors to open. There was a concerted, but silent rush as the spectators took their seats.

Bruce Richard Spence was called to the stand. He was asked by the District Attorney to state his job title and duties.

"I'm employed by the Oklahoma State Bureau of Investigation in Oklahoma City and my job title is crime scene senior specialist. My duties are primarily in the area of fingerprint work. I can classify, search and file latent fingerprints on articles of evidence and I can compare latent prints with known fingerprints."

"How long have you been engaged in this particular discipline?"

"I have been with the Bureau for thirteen years and in fingerprint work for approximately seven years."

Asked about his educational training and experience, Spence answered, detailing his experience and number of FBI schools attended. When asked to estimate the number of times he had had occasion to make fingerprint comparisons, Spence could only respond that it was in the course of everyday work since 1981. He had done a very large number of cases in that length of time.

For the benefit of the court, the District Attorney asked for a definition of the word latent fingerprint.

"The word latent means hidden. And a latent print is a print left behind when an individual touches an object. It is usually invisible to the naked eye and rendered fully visible by the application of various powders or chemicals."

Then Anderson directed him to observe State's Exhibit number 48. Spence stepped down from the witness box to do so. After resuming his seat, Anderson asked him to give the particulars about the evidence.

"I saw this at the OSBI central laboratory, which is in Oklahoma City, and it was shown to me by criminalist Mary Long."

Through questions and answers, Spence gave the information that several prints were examined and photographed. They were marked State's Exhibit 50 and 51. Spence described the process by which the print is under five power magnification and the individual details that comprise a fingerprint. Then he explained that the two prints to be compared are laid side by side so that the ending ridge, a dividing ridge, a ridge consisting of a series of dots, maybe a short ridge, a ridge with a little island or enclosure in the center of it, all these things are compared. The same unique characteristics in the same place on the same ridge in both fingerprints.

He told the courtroom, "When I can find eight of these unique characteristics that match up with none which do not match up, then I have effected identification."

He was asked if State's Exhibit 49 was submitted to him for examination and he replied that it was.

"Based on your comparison, do you have an opinion concerning the identity of the fingerprints which appear on State's Exhibit 50 and 51 with those prints that appear on State's 49?"

"Yes, sir, I do have an opinion. The latent prints, State's Exhibit's 50 and 51 are identical in ridge detail to the impression which appears in block number six, indicated for the left thumb on the finger print card, State's Exhibit 49."

When asked about the other fingerprints on the door, Spence was unable to come to a conclusive opinion.

Anderson said solemnly, "Your Honor, at this time, the State and Counsel for the Defendant Stepp have entered into a stipulation for purposes of this Preliminary Hearing only. We would stipulate as fact that State's Exhibit Number 49 is the fingerprint card bearing the fingerprints of Francine Stepp."

Then it was the defense attorneys chance to cross-examine and try to reduce the impact and damage to the defendants' case of the bloody fingerprint.

Bowyer briskly walked up to the witness and asked, "Please tell the court how many prints you attempted to lift off this door glass?"

"There were approximately four or five separate impressions which I had photographed."

Bowyer questioned him about the ridge detail and then asked why Spence had not once mentioned the Henry method of identifying fingerprints. "Could you please tell the Court about the Henry system and the full system, including the loops, arches and swirls besides the ridges?"

Spence responded, "The Henry system is a system of classifying a series of fingerprints according to their pattern types. It is called the Henry system after its developer, Sir Edward Henry, who was a British consulate stationed in India around the turn of the century. Utilizing the Henry system of classification in filing fingerprints, it is possible to identify an individual by fingerprints alone without regard to name. And if a set of fingerprints with no name whatsoever are given to me, I can classify them by this system and search them through a file which has been filed by the Henry system. I can come up with an identical set of prints, if there is one in there.

"Mr. Bowyer mentioned arches and loops and the term he used was swirls. The correct term is whorl, spelling w-h-o-r-l. Now, those are the three basic pattern types which are found within the Henry system. And what it involves is very simply going through each print on the card one at a time, identifying it as a plain arch or a tinted arch, as an owner loop or a radial loop, or as a whorl of any one of four different varieties and then using that information to build a formula by which a fingerprint card may be filed in a specific position within the Henry classification file."

Spence sat back in his chair with a trace of a smile.

Bowyer demanded, "Did you find any loops or whorls in these fingerprints?"

"As I recall, the one that I identified is a loop."

"It was not mentioned on direct examination, just ridges." Then, changing tactics, he asked, "Could you tell the court how long these fingerprints had been on the door?"

"I don't know how long they had been on the door, sir."

"These other fingerprints that you have photographed, are all of them from the inside of the door? Is that correct?"

"Yes, sir."

"And the ones that have been marked and introduced State's Exhibit 50 and 52, are both of those in the region up to about a quarter way down on the right hand side on the inside of the glass?"

"Yes, sir."

Spence was asked why he did not lift any fingerprints from the latch area of the door and he responded because he didn't see any there. Then Bowyer asked how many fingerprints of the other residents of the house Spence had been able to identify. Mark Stepp's palm print apparently was taken from the bedroom window. Bowyer pointed out that fingerprints would be all over the house, if a person resided in that house.

"Were the fingerprints put on this glass with force? Lightly? Were they streaked or was it simply someone laying their hand against the glass to make the impression?"

"The impressions that I photographed were not streaked or smudged. When that happens, we lose the ridge detail and the print is not of value to us. As to the amount of force or as to the circumstances around which the print was put on the surface, of course, I don't know anything about that. I can't tell anything about the amount of force just from looking at the print."

Bowyer asked a few more questions about perspiration and body oils, and then concluded by getting the witness to repeat that he did not know under what circumstances the fingerprints were placed on the door.

Ms. Ramsey asked if there were items in the serology lab and photography lab that had been analyzed. Spence replied that Mary Long would be in charge of the serology lab items and Bill Pickle, photographer would have those items.

Then Anderson asked questions on redirect.

"There is one matter I want to clear up. There were, in fact a number of latent fingerprints that you examined that related to one defendant, correct?"

"That is correct."

"Approximately how many regular fingerprints or latent fingerprints related to one of the defendants in this case, according to your report?"

"Well, in addition to the one I have testified to, according to the report, I have got approximately forty-seven latent prints pertaining to one defendant."

Anderson said, "But there was only one bloody print that you were able to identify; is that correct?"

Bowyer leapt up, objecting, "Your Honor, that is leading and suggestive."

Judge Belden sustained that objection, so Anderson rephrased his question.

"Was there a bloody print?"

"There was a print which was enhanced by a chemical which I understand is a presumptive test for blood."

"But the other forty-seven prints were regular latent prints, correct?"

Spence answered precisely, "Most of those others were developed with a chemical called Ninhydrin."

"And those prints were identified as belonging to whom, the forty-seven?"

As Spence started to talk, Bowyer objected again. "He hasn't laid the proper foundation, Your Honor."

Obviously irritated, Anderson responded, "I am just asking him if he made comparisons of the prints. They are looking at the same report I am. I gave it to them a long time ago. I don't know what the objection is."

"I will stand on my objection."

Anderson finally managed to obtain the information he was seeking: that the forty-seven latent prints were made by the same individual who made the fingerprints on State's Exhibit 49, namely Francine Stepp, but only one print was enhanced with orthotoluidine.

On recross, Bowyer asked, "Mr. Spence, a normal individual, such as yourself that lives at your residence in a normal day, how many fingerprints do you put in your own house in a single day?"

"I would have no idea."

Bowyer pushed further with this idea, "It could be forty-seven or a hundred and forty-seven, couldn't it?"

"Like I say, I don't know, sir."

"But forty-seven prints for a person that lives in that house is very normal?"

Now it was Anderson objecting, "Your Honor, we are not offering the forty-seven prints. We just tried to distinguish there was only one that was a bloody print. We are not offering the forty-seven prints. It is very natural, since they live there. We are not arguing that."

The Judge agreed, "All right."

Bowyer protested, "That might be very true, Your Honor, but the test is…"

Judge Belden spoke firmly, "But he has asked and answered your question, that particular question."

Bowyer then went on to ask what other items besides the door was supplied to make comparisons on, and was told there was a complete list in the report. Then he asked whose fingerprints, besides Mark Stepp's palm print were identified.

"Besides the decedents, there were Cindy Wynn's, Fred Rank, and there may have been one other individual whose name I can't recall without looking at the report."

"Did you find any prints that were not identified?"

"Yes, sir."

"Do you know to this day who those prints belong to?"

"I have no idea, sir."

Then he was asked if there were any fingerprints on the .22 rifle, and he responded that there were none. Then Bowyer indicated he was through and the court was recessed for another day.

Chapter Seven

In presenting the State's case to the Court, DA Anderson proceeded by calling Mike Reed to the stand. The detectives knew the young man's testimony was crucial, and hoped that he would make the same strong statements to the court that he had told them, but they were apprehensive. They had both seen confident, truthful witnesses disintegrate into faltering, hesitant testifiers totally discredited from the efforts of a skillful cross-examiner. And they knew this young man was scared and nervous at the start.

Asked to state his name, his answer was so soft Anderson asked him to speak up. Then he gave his age, nineteen years, and his address in Stillwater. When asked if he knew any of the people sitting at the front table, he replied in the affirmative.

Anderson asked, "For the purposes of the record, which one is Francine Stepp?"

"The redhead right there." Mike pointed to Francine, who still kept her head lowered, not meeting his eyes. Then they went through the same process identifying Cindy Wynn. Cindy tossed her head and looked at him, smiling with her mouth closed.

Anderson elicited the information that Mike had come

to Stillwater from Pine Bluff, Arkansas four or five months previously to live with his father and stepmother.

"And who was living in your dad's home at that time?"

"Cindy Wynn and my stepbrother and my stepmother and my dad."

"Was she boarding with your dad or being allowed to stay there?"

"She was like paying board, paying my dad, I think, twenty five dollars a week to stay with us."

"What portion of the house do you sleep in?"

"Downstairs in the den on a couch bed."

"And Cindy Wynn had a room that she rented, and where was that room?"

"Right next to—Cindy's room was right next to my bed. It was downstairs where I slept."

Anderson brought out the testimony that Francine had visited the house several times. Then he asked about a specific conversation between Mike and the defendants.

Both Ramsey and Bowyer objected, and Anderson went back to establish a proper foundation.

The conversation had occurred at his parents house in the living room about noon, but he could not be exact about the date, other than a couple of months before the murders had taken place. Besides the defendants and himself there was another young man present named Jackie Myers.

. Then Anderson was ready to tackle the actual conversation.

"What did Cindy say at this conversation?"

"She said she was going to take care of Francine's parents."

"How did she describe that?"

"She didn't actually describe it. She just said she was going to get even with them."

"Why did she say she was going to get even with them?"

"Because Francine's parents wouldn't let Cindy hang around with her."

"At this conversation did Francine Stepp make any comments?"

"She just said, 'Hi' to me."

"Was there anything else said that you recall at that conversation?"

"Just that they offered Jackie a big sum of money to help them."

"To help them do what?"

"To help them take care of Francine's parents."

"Did you ever have another conversation with these two defendants, Cindy Wynn and Francine Stepp?"

"I didn't have it, but they was upstairs and I overheard it."

Bowyer objected and the objection was sustained. Anderson tried to elicit information concerning the second conversation and this time the Court allowed him to answer what he overheard.

Anderson established that this conversation had taken place two or three days after the first one.

"What were these two defendants talking about?"

"Taking care of Francine's parents."

"One at a time, what did Cindy say?"

"That they would go in and do the job and that they would send Francine back in later, that they would drive around a little bit about a couple hours and then they would send Francine back in to play it all off like nothing happened."

"At this second conversation, did Francine say anything?"

"Not much."

There was a recess then of ten minutes.

Bowyer knew as he got up to cross-examine, he needed to damage the witness' credibility. Mike Reed had come across as a nice, nervous young man who was determined to tell the truth.

"Mr. Reed, within the past ten years, have you ever been convicted of a felony?"

"Yes, sir."

"And what is that?"

"When I was fourteen, I was accused of molesting a little boy."

"Within the past ten years, have you ever been convicted of a misdemeanor involving theft or dishonesty?"

"No."

"And where was the molestation? Where was that filed at?"

The District Attorney objected. "I did not oppose it because I did not wish to hide it, but this is a juvenile matter. It is not a felony. I would state for the record he was charged in juvenile court and it was not a felony. And other than the revelation of it, I would object to any further questions by counsel."

The Judge agreed, and the witness, far from being discredited, revealed himself as being painfully truthful, even though he was not very knowledgeable about terminology and charges.

Bowyer questioned Reed about his past residence in Arkansas and asked if his father was in the courtroom that day. He was told the father was sitting outside the door, which is usual when the person may be called to testify, to prevent them from hearing the previous testimony.

Then Bowyer asked, "You say you've had contact with Francine Stepp, had some sort of talk or communications or whatever?"

"I didn't talk much to Francine."

"Did she talk to you?"

"She would say 'Hi' and 'How am I doing' and stuff like that."

Bowyer had the young man go over the same ground, giving his father's address and relating how long he'd lived there and how long ago he'd met the defendants.

"Now, could you tell the Court how big this house is?"

"How big it is?"

"Do you know the square footage of the house?"

"I couldn't tell you."

"Could you tell the Court how many rooms or bedrooms this house has?"

"It's got two bedrooms, a den and big basement."

There was testimony about the placement of the rooms, the beds and the couch and the couch bed.

"Now, getting precisely to the point in time where you overheard some conversation between Cindy Wynn and other individuals, where were you at in the house?"

"In the living room, sitting on a chair with them."

At that time Bowyer requested the use of an easel and paper be provided so that the witness could draw where he was located and everything else.

The slender, tall youth walked to the easel and said as he drew, "This is the living room and there's a chair."

"Excuse me just a moment, sir. Just for purposes of getting this, can you draw the house where it sets in the streets and the intersections?"

"No, I sure can't."

"Can you draw the approximate, without to scale, the floor plan of the upper, the lower and the basement of this house on the same sheet of paper?"

Anderson objected, "I'm not real sure what the relevancy of the floor plan and the pitch of the roof and a lot of those other details has to do with his testimony. I would have no objection if he draws a big square and would identify where everybody was present in the room, but if the conversation took place in one room, I would object to the relevancy of the floor plan of the rest of the house."

Bowyer answered, "In response to that, Your Honor, there has been, I don't believe, any testimony as to where specifically these two conversations took place. I have no idea at this time whether they took place at the same place or they took place in the same room or they took place on the same floor of this residence."

Ms. Ramsey spoke then, "Your Honor, on behalf of Defendant Wynn, there was testimony with regard to where the conversation took place, one being in the living room which he attempted to draw earlier where everyone was present, and further there was a conversation that took place in a bedroom that he overheard but was not present. And I think the floor plan would be helpful in knowing where he was located at the time he overheard this other conversation, whether or not he could hear and how far he was away and things of that nature and request that he be allowed to make that drawing."

Anderson interjected, "I want to correct. What he did say was that he was not a part of the conversation. He was present in the room. That's what he said."

Bowyer argued, "We believe the record would speak for itself, Your Honor."

Judge Belden declared, "At this time the last question you asked him was about the conversation that took place in the living room. Do you want a diagram about that where the parties were present?"

Anderson replied, "We would have no objection to drawing a big X, labeling it living room and being asked to respond to questions where people were seated or any other activity that took place."

Bowyer requested that the witness draw where the first conversation had taken place.

Again, Mike took the marker in his hand and spoke while he was drawing. "Okay. This is the living room. There is a door right there. That there is a big couch when you first walk through, and then my dad's room is right over here to the left, and then there is a love seat and there's a chair right over here. Cindy was sitting on the couch and I think Francine was sitting over here on the love seat and they was talking like I told you."

The witness was asked about the time of day, which he answered as being about noon and the exact day, which he could not recall. Then Bowyer asked him if Cindy and Francine invited him into the living room, where they were.

"No, I lived there. Why would they invite me in for?"

"Okay, now whenever you walked into the room, how many people were in this room?"

"Three." And he named them again.

The court was recessed for noon and the Judge cautioned the witness not to discuss his testimony with anyone during the lunch hour.

Continuing the cross examination after lunch, Bowyer asked the witness if he recalled that they were at the point of being in the living room. Again he was asked if he could pinpoint the date and he replied that he could not.

"Was this in the morning or in the afternoon?"

"About twelve noon because I had just got off work."

Each person in the diagrammed living room, represented by a number was circled and labeled at the bottom of the page with that person's name.

He was asked the position of each person, and he answered that Cindy was seated on the couch, Francine was seated on the love seat and Jackie was lying on the floor.

He was asked to estimate the distance in feet from each person, which he did, estimating between five and ten feet between each person.

Bowyer asked if a radio or television or ceiling fan was on in the room at the time of the conversation and was told there was no ceiling fan in the room and Mike didn't remember if the TV was on.

"Can you tell the court, if any, what noise was in this room besides the individuals talking?"

"My dad's fish tank."

He obliged Francine's counsel by marking on the drawing where the fish tank was located.

"While this conversation was taking place, did anyone else enter the room?"

"My stepbrother did once, but he went back upstairs in two or three minutes."

"Initially, sir, when you first came into the room, what was everyone's response in the room. Were they shocked or continued along what they were doing?"

"Cindy and Francine and Jackie just told me 'Hi' and they just continued on talking."

"What did you overhear at this time."

"Like I said, Cindy and Francine was talking about getting rid of Francine's parents. They was—Cindy was mad at Francine's parents because Francine's parents wouldn't let Cindy hang around with her, go out with her or something like that."

"You've stated 'getting rid of'. Is that as close as you recall about—"

"That's all that they said."

Reed didn't know who initiated the conversation about Francine's parents because he said he walked into the middle of it. When asked how long the conversation went on, he replied about thirty minutes.

Asked to be specific, he continued, "Francine and Jackie and Cindy were talking about getting rid of Francine's parents and they offered Jackie a big sum of money to help them."

Bowyer asked, "Who offered the money, sir?"

"Cindy."

"You say a 'big sum'. Could you please tell the Court what a big sum is?"

"I don't remember the exact amount, but it was a lot of money."

"And this was the sole content of the conversation for the thirty minutes while you were in the room?" Bowyer's skepticism was evident in his tone of voice.

"Yes, sir, it sure was."

"Nothing else was talked about except this?"

"No there wasn't."

"Sir, I ask you this point blank. Do you remember Francine Stepp saying anything about her being involved in a murder?"

"Francine did not say nothing about it."

"Did you think that these people were serious about this conversation?"

"No, sir, I sure didn't. They was mad."

"Excuse me?"

"They was mad with Francine's parents. We just blew it off."

"A prank, a joke?"

"We thought Cindy was just joking around."

"Blowing off steam?"

"Yeah, everybody does it."

"At any time during this conversation, did anyone request you to be involved in it?"

"No, sir."

"Did anybody, this Jackie Myers, Cindy Wynn, or Francine Stepp immediately prior to you walking out say, 'Don't tell this to anybody?'"

"No, sir."

"Did they greet you goodbye when you left?"

"I went to take a shower. I just got off work. They didn't say nothing to me."

Then the witness was directed to use a clean sheet of paper and draw where each person was during the second conversation.

"Was your fish tank still in the room, pumping and bubbling, whatever it does?"

"Yes."

"Now at this time, they were already in the room and you walked in?"

"Yes."

"What did you overhear?"

"Francine and Cindy planning to kill Francine's parents."

"Was any mention made during this conversation on how?"

"No."

"Now again, sir, we weren't there, so please, if you will, from your own opinion, was there a lot of joking and laughter going on?"

"No. They were still mad, but there wasn't no laughing or joking."

He was asked again why they were mad at Francine's parents and he explained it was because they didn't want Cindy hanging around Francine. He was asked his whereabouts the night of the murder and he replied at home with his parents.

Then Bowyer started asking about the police officers who questioned him.

"Okay. When they came out to you sir, in your opinion, did they come out there and ask you questions about a conversation that took place, or did they come out and there and say, 'We've got the people that did it, we want to know if you were involved in it?'"

"They come out and asked me about a conversation that took place."

"Okay. In this asking you about a conversation, it's true is it not, that the police officers were supplying you the information about what took place and you simply agreed with them?"

Anderson objected, "Your Honor, that kind of asked the question and answered it in the same question. That is no question. That's my objection. I object to the form of the question. It's leading."

The Judge stated, "Well, if the witness understands it, I'll let him answer it."

"I don't understand what you mean."

Bowyer said, "When the police officers—I'll move on, Your Honor."

Emphatically, the Judge said, "Good."

"When the police officers came out, did you feel in your own opinion they were asking you questions or were they putting words in your mouth?"

"They was asking me questions."

Bowyer learned that the questioning by the police had lasted about ten or fifteen minutes. The witness stated that he did not sign anything or write anything, but that the policemen made notes about what he was saying.

"Did they indicate to you at that time that you might be coming to court to testify?"

"They said there was a good possibility that I might have to come."

He was asked to name the officers and point them out, but he only knew one of them by his first name. He replied to an inquiry that the police had not told him anything he didn't know.

"Was there anything else in the conversation discussed between Cindy and Francine which you overheard that you have not told me and the Court about here today?"

"Just that they was going to go in and do it and that then they was going to send Francine back in a few hours later and she was going to play it off like nothing happened."

"I ask you this, sir. From the opinion that you formed at that time, who was going to go in and do it?"

"They never did say."

Then Bowyer wanted to know who he had told about these conversations and the information given revealed that he had told five of his co-workers, his father, stepbrother and his mother. He related that he was afraid to testify in court and that he had told Jackie Myers, who had also been subpoenaed, that he was scared. When asked if they got together and compared stories he denied it emphatically.

Bowyer concluded his cross-examination and then it was Ms. Ramsey's turn to cross examine.

Her questions were similar to Bowyer's, emphasizing the fact the witness thought the conversations were a joke.

"Did they specifically say why they were mad?"

"Because Francine's parents wouldn't let Cindy hang around with Francine."

"Were they together at the time?"

"Yes."

"Did you see them together at other times?"

"They were sneaking around behind Francine's parents."

"They were sneaking around behind their backs?"

"Right."

Ms. Ramsey focused then on the money, asking where the witness thought the defendants would get a large sum of money to pay Jackie Myers. He replied that he took it as a joke.

Again the time of the conversation was questioned but Mike was positive about the time frame, since he had just gotten off work. There was no shaking his testimony. Ms. Ramsey brought out by questioning that the defendants had not made any effort to keep the conversation secret from anyone. He did not recall who started the conversation, and he steadfastly refused to say anything different from his previous testimony. There was a discussion on what the witness would consider a large sum of money, until Anderson objected, "Your Honor. I think we could go in increments of $50 and be here all night. That's a point to be argued. If he doesn't know, he doesn't know. That's kind of like when it is too hot; when is it too cold."

The Court sustained the objection. Ms. Ramsey asked what his relationship was with Cindy.

"I look at Cindy like a sister. Me and my stepbrother called her Sis all the time."

"Did you ever have a crush on her?"

"I sure did."

"And did she owe your father any money?"

"She paid him the $25 a week, but on the last, she didn't pay him."

"So she still owes your father money."

"Yes, Ma'am."

When asked about Francine, he replied he didn't know her that well. He testified that no one was using alcoholic beverages or doing drugs when these conversations were taking place.

"You did not contact the police and volunteer this information to them is that correct?"

"No, Ma'am."

"And you have not seen Cindy since the time she was arrested; is that correct?"

"Yes, Ma'am."

"Did you ever see Miss Wynn in the custody of a gun at any time?"

"No, Ma'am."

Ms. Ramsey concluded her cross-examination and DA Anderson asked on redirect, "I have one question. A moment ago, Mr. Reed, the question was asked whether you had ever seen Miss Wynn with a firearm and I think your answer was no."

"Yes, sir."

"Directing your attention to this conversation, both conversations that you heard, was there any discussion of a knife or a weapon or bullets or any other type of a weapon?"

"She wanted to know where she could find a gun."

"Let's stop right there. We have two defendants. I want you first to tell me that statement you made, did you hear it during the first conversation or during the second conversation?"

"First."

"And when you said she asked about a gun, who are you talking about?"

"Cindy."

"And what did she say?"

"She wanted to know where she could find a gun."

"And to whom did she ask that question?"

"To anybody that would answer it."

"Did anybody respond?"

"I didn't."

"Did anyone respond? Did you hear anyone respond?"

"No, sir, I sure didn't."

"Was there any other conversation by either defendant concerning a weapon or bullets or anything?"

"None that I recall. They just wanted to know where they could find one."

Bowyer jumped to his feet. "Objection, Your Honor. That's not what he just got through testifying to just a moment ago. It was that Cindy Wynn was asking about a gun, not they."

The Judge noted that it was a different response.

Anderson said, "The point is well taken. Do you understand what Council is saying? A moment ago you said Cindy said it, and now you are saying they. It's very important that you tell the Court and the counsel who made that statement. Cindy or Francine?"

"Cindy made the statement."

"That's all."

Ms. Ramsey on recross examination tried to repair the damage.

"Was this during the same conversation where everything was a joke?"

"Yes, Ma'am."

"And what did she say?"

"She really didn't say. She just wanted to know where she could get one."

"Where she could get a gun. She didn't even have one, did she?"

"No, Ma'am. Not that I knew of."

"And this was part of the continuing joke?"

"Yes, Ma'am. We took it as a joke, like a joke."

"No further questions, Your Honor."

Then the witness was allowed to step down. The police officers sagged in their seats with relief. This young man with the ninth grade education had performed on the witness stand better than some college graduates they'd seen.

Chapter Eight

District Attorney Anderson called Dennis McGrath to the stand. He was duly sworn and stated his name, rank and position in the Stillwater Police Department as investigator.

"How long have you been employed by the Stillwater Police Department?"

"Approximately seven years."

"In connection with the investigation of the homicides of Mark and Delores Stepp, did you have occasion to interview either of the defendants?"

"Yes, I did."

"Beginning with Francine Stepp, when did you first interview her?"

"The morning of the 8th of June, 1988."

"And do you recall the conversation at that time?"

"At that time, the only information that was gained was at about midnight or twelve thirty, she had returned to the residence to pick up a change of clothes, went to the residence and left. And then about six or six thirty that morning she went home and found her parents."

The counsel for the defense asked the location of this interview and it was clarified that it took place at the Wynn residence, next door to the Stepp residence.

Later in the day, McGrath testified that Francine had come to the police station. At that time she had been read the adult Miranda Rights form, a copy of which was then handed to her and she was asked to initial it with the date.

The defense counsel asked several questions about the Miranda rights, and Ms. Ramsey agreed to stipulate the contents of the Miranda Rights form, rather than having them read into the court's records. Bowyer said, "It will just be one question."

Heaving a small sigh, the Judge said, "All right. Go ahead and ask the question."

"Detective McGrath, did you ask Francine Stepp whether she could read?"

"No, sir."

Bowyer than objected to the admission.

The DA asked, "Were the five enumerated items *read* to her on State's Exhibit Number 52?"

"Yes, sir."

The initialed copy was admitted into evidence without objection for purposes of Preliminary Hearing from Ms. Ramsey, but the fact Bowyer still objected was noted.

Anderson asked McGrath what Francine said about the events that had occurred at her parent's home.

"She stated that she had gotten off work at OSU at approximately nine. When she got off work, she went to a friend's house. From there, her and the friend both went back to her house. She stayed there for a little while. Her and the friend left. It was about eleven thirty, twelve o'clock. At about twelve thirty, they went riding around. They went back to her friend's house and they stayed there.

Later on during that same interview, she provided a little bit more detail as to what transpired through the course of the evening. At about nine o'clock, she got off work, went home, straight home from work. She received a phone call from a boyfriend, a Mr. Fred Rank, stayed there and ate supper and then went to Cindy Wynn's apartment on High Point. They stayed there until about eleven thirty and then returned to Francine's parents' house with Cindy. They talked with the parents about a softball tournament and about Francine spending the night with Cindy and her mother said it was okay, as long as she was back early in the morning. They then went back to the apartment on High Point and stayed there until about six o'clock."

"Who did? Who went back?"

"Cindy and Francine."

"What else was said?"

"Later on, she provided that when they left the house at about ten o'clock she went to Cindy's, drove around town and Boomer Lake, talked to some of Cindy's friends at the lake, went back to Francine's at about eleven and then left Francine's and drove around the lake and returned to Francine's for about thirty to forty-five minutes to pick up a change of clothes. After she did that, she went back to the apartment on High Point and stayed there until about six, at which time she went home and found her parents."

"Did you on that day have occasion to visit with the defendant, Cindy Wynn?"

"Yes, sir, I did."

He stated that the conversation took place at two thirty in the afternoon, June 8th at the Stillwater Police Department. In response to further questions about Francine, he stated that Francine Stepp was not in custody at that time and that she had left after the interview.

As McGrath started to testify about Cindy Wynn's interview, Ms. Ramsey objected that they didn't know if she had been admonished of her Miranda warnings.

Anderson frowned and explained that at this particular time, Miranda Warnings are only required in custodial interrogation. As far as they knew Ms. Wynn was considered to be a witness, but certainly not considered anything else, therefore no Miranda warnings were given.

At the district attorney's direction to proceed, McGrath continued, "At about nine o'clock the previous evening, Francine came by to Cindy Wynn's apartment at 802 High Point. At about nine thirty, Francine, Cindy and her boyfriend, a Randy Jackson, departed the apartment together and proceeded downstairs. Once they got downstairs, Mr. Jackson proceeded to walk off to another destination that he was going to. Cindy and Francine drove away. They drove around town for a little while. After riding around for some time, Francine asked Cindy if she could spend the night with her.

"At about ten-thirty, they went back to Francine's house to tell her parents that she was going to spend the night with Cindy and let her parents know where she would be. When they got there, they didn't see the parents, so they departed. At about midnight, according to Ms. Wynn, Randy got home. Cindy and Francine went back to the house to get Cindy's cigarettes and some change that she had left on the counter at the Stepp residence. At that time, according to Ms. Wynn, her parents were in bed and she has no idea what Francine was doing. They did both go into the house together.

"At about five minutes past two a.m. on the 8th, Cindy and Francine arrived back at 802 High Point and sat and talked. They got up about three o'clock and proceeded to Jack Griffith's and got a coke and went back to 802 High Point and set the alarm for six thirty and proceeded to go to sleep.

"At six-thirty, the alarm went off and Francine got up, got dressed and left. Francine at that time told Cindy and Randy she would be back at about nine o'clock. At about ten o'clock Francine hadn't shown up and Cindy tried to call her, apparently to no avail."

"Any other comments made by Defendant Wynn at that time?"

"Other than to the effect that Francine had been with her through the whole course of the night, as far as she knew, she hadn't left Cindy's or Randy's apartment during the course of the night. Everything she recounted was in the company of Ms. Stepp."

Anderson concluded, "That's all I have." The Court asked defense counsels, "Any cross-examination? Do you wish to reserve cross-examination?" Both defense attorneys' made a statement to reserve their cross-examination on this witness.

Then the district attorney called Billy Bartram to the stand. In response to questions, he stated his name, the fact that he had been employed by the Stillwater Police Department for eight years in the capacity of detective sergeant.

There was more objection to testimony from defense counsels regarding Miranda warnings. Again, Anderson stated that the defendant was not in custody and asked if she had come to the Police Headquarters under restraint. Bartram testified that she came of her own free will and left at the conclusion of the interview.

"What questions and what responses were given?"

"I asked for some hair samples. She gave some hair samples after being read a consent."

"What else?"

"I questioned her in regard to discrepancies made in her statement. She responded that she had gone home at approximately ten forty-five p.m. Her mother and father were there. She told them that she was—she spoke with them about spending the night with Cindy."

Anderson asked, "And she said she saw her parents there?"

"She said she spoke with her mother and father about spending the night with Cindy and that she had left and came back home around eleven thirty or twelve o'clock that same night to change clothes and remove her contact lenses.

"She didn't say anything about her contacts, I believe, in any other interviews that anybody has advised me of. She was asked why she did not mention anything about the contacts before. She replied that she didn't know. She also said that she didn't change clothes when she went home at eleven thirty, which was one of the reasons for going home. In response to what kind of clothes she had on at that time, she said that, as best she could remember, she had on an Eskimo Joe's shirt and that it should have been in the grey truck. The jeans that she would have been wearing was the pair that she had had on, however they had been washed numerous times. Her footwear at that time or on that particular evening on June 7th would have been boots.

"During the time that we were interviewing her, she was showing some emotions as far as her breathing pattern wasn't consistent. She had rapid and shallow breath. She was clutching her hands so tight together her knuckles were turning white. We confronted her with the interview that we had conducted of a neighbor, Ms. Laura Samples, about her driving a black Camaro. She denied that she had been in a black Camaro that night. She also denied driving down Marie Street, which was the street on the west side of her residence. She stated when she left, the majority of the time, she would turn back east, in an easterly direction up Rogers Drive and then turn and go back down south, down Audene. When she was asked about why an independent witness not involved in this investigation had given that statement, the only reply she could give was that she probably was not liked and somebody wanted to see her get in trouble.

"She was also questioned about any activity that she participated in along with her family in regards to any nudist activities during any of their vacations."

Bowyer threw his head back, "What was that?"

"Nudist activities".

Bartram continued, "She had advised Investigator Mc-Grath during their initial interview that she did not participate in that type activity. However, during the crime scene investigation at the house on June 8th, there were photographs found depicting Mrs. Stepp and Francine Stepp in the nude playing with some type of plastic, black plastic that had been wetted down to resemble a Slip 'N Slide. She was asked about that and stated that she had participated only when there were not other people around. She was also questioned about any type of sexual activity with her family and she said that she had never had any type of that activity.

"She was also questioned in regards to a statement that was made by Cindy Wynn, who stated a couple of days after the murder that Francine and her boyfriend, Fred Rank, had come over to her house at 821 High Point. She and Francine were sitting in the breezeway of the apartment complex talking and Cindy had stated she noticed scratch marks on..."

Bartram was interrupted by Bowyer's objection. "This is hearsay at this point."

The objection was sustained.

DA Anderson asked, "Are these statements that were given by Francine?"

Bartram replied, "These are statements that—I'm confronting Francine at this point with these statements that were made to me by Cindy Wynn."

Anderson explained, "At this point, it would probably involve hearsay, so I would ask you at this time to give only Ms. Stepp's response."

"Ms. Stepp stated she didn't know why Cindy would say anything like that and the only reason she could think of was because she wanted to get her in trouble. It appeared during the conversation that when Francine Stepp was confronted with any type of conflicting statement, the only logical statement she could come up with..."

Again, Bowyer objected, "That calls for a conclusion of the witness."

It was sustained.

"Would you limit your remarks to what was said by Francine Stepp?"

"Every time she answered a question, it was with the response, somebody wanted to get her into trouble."

Then the District Attorney moved on to the night of July 12, when Bartram interviewed Francine at Police Headquarters. Nothing new was brought out in this questioning, except the fact that Francine was not read her rights at that time, since she was not in custody, and that she terminated the interview by getting up and leaving Bartram's office. Both defense counsels reserved the right to cross-examine the witness later.

District Attorney Anderson had skillfully built his case much like a builder, laying the foundation, the mortar binding it together and now for the finishing touch, he called Lieutenant Ronald Thrasher.

Lieutenant Thrasher answered to his questions that he was commander of the criminal investigation division, and had been employed by the Stillwater Police Department for ten years.

The District Attorney then asked, if in connection with investigating the crime, he had interviewed Francine Stepp. Thrasher replied that on July 12, he had spoken with her, after she had been fingerprinted and after she had spoken with Sgt. Bartram.

"I began by talking to her. I told her that the interview that we were having at that time, as previous interviews, had all been videotaped and she indicated that she knew that. I told her that I had spoken with her grandfather and her aunt and had told them of the available evidence we had in the case at that time. I told her that I thought that she was deeply involved in the situation and we talked about Sergeant Bartram."

"What other remarks did she make to you?"

"I told her that Sergeant Bartram had an appointment to speak with the District Attorney on the following Friday and at that time, his plans were to present a case and to request that the District Attorney file a charge in this case. And I showed her a time log chart that we, the investigators, had prepared that detailed interviews and information that was given in interviews at different times. I told her that I did not believe that she had been totally honest with investigators in the case. Then I went into some of the evidence that we had and told her about that evidence and asked her if she would like to tell me what had happened on the day that she had reported the death of her parents."

"Did she respond?"

"Yes, sir, she did."

"What was the first thing that she said in connection with the deaths of her parents?"

Bowyer asserted, "Your Honor, at this time, I will renew my motion under the Miranda decision. I would also state that I know the Court is taking it under advisement, but I would state that at this point that argument will proceed on psychological coercion from the Police Department; that she was in custody. For the purpose of the record, I would cite *White versus State, 674 P.2d 31.* Also the Fourteenth Amendment of the Constitution of the United States of America. Also Article II, Section 20 from the Constitution of the State of Oklahoma and request that testimony from this point forward be suppressed and the Court will take that under advisement. I am just, for purposes of the record, making my objection."

Judge Belden said, "All right. It is noted in the record."

The DA Anderson turned back to Lieutenant Thrasher and reminded him they were at the point where Francine was starting to tell him what happened on the day she reported her parents' deaths.

"She said that she went in the front door that morning and left through the front door. She went into detail and said that after she went through the front door she had gone into her bedroom. Then she went to her parents' bedroom and then left through the front door. At that time, I told her that Sergeant Bartram would relay or report any cooperation that she gave us in the investigation to the District Attorney when presenting the case.

"She then said that she didn't know what she was supposed to say or, correction, she did not know what she was supposed to have thrown out of her car and that she wasn't even driving her car that night. About that time, it was just shortly after seven o'clock and we took a break in the interview. Her aunt came in and then later her grandfather. At about seven thirty, I came back into the room and the interview continued at that time."

"At any time during the second interview, did you apprise her of what we have referred to as Miranda rights?"

"Yes, sir, I did."

"Let's begin with the second interview, and I want you to tell me what was said and I want you to tell me at what part of the interview the Miranda warnings were read to her and how they were read to her."

"At about seven thirty or shortly thereafter, I came back into the room and her aunt and grandfather left. This was after her grandfather told me that she wanted to talk to me again. She first said that everybody hated her and then I asked her if the gun that we found in the house was the gun that shot her parents and she said that it was not the rifle, that it was her father's pistol and that it was in Boomer Lake up by the dam."

Bowyer renewed his objection.

"And at that time, I left the room."

"And did you return?"

"Yes, about eight, I came back into the room and read her the Miranda rights."

The card, dated and initialed was marked State's Exhibit 53, after both defense counsels stipulated to what the card says. Bowyer asked Thrasher, as he had asked McGrath previously, if he had asked Francine if she could read. Lieutenant Thrasher said he had not, since she was able to write.

"Did she make any further statements concerning the homicide of her parents?"

"She said that Cindy had thrown the gun in the lake on the east end of the dam and that between nine thirty and ten o'clock, Cindy and her had gone over to Francine's house. She said that they had talked with her parents that evening and Fred, Francine's boyfriend, had called and at about midnight her parents had gone to bed.

"Cindy and her, when asked, indicated that they had planned the murder just that morning. She stated that when her parents went to bed that she had gone out through the garage to get Cindy, who was lying out in the woods. She said that the gun was upstairs in Francine's room at that time. She stated that she had gotten the gun earlier that day and then later said that afternoon.

"Francine said that she got Cindy and that they had both returned to the house up to her room and that at that time, the gun was already loaded. She stated that they walked downstairs and at that time, Cindy had the gun. They walked to the bedroom door. Francine was supposed to kick in the bedroom door, but Cindy decided at that time that she didn't want to do it. She stated that they went to another room and talked and that Cindy wanted Francine to do it. Cindy stated, according to Francine, that it is either now or never. They went back to the bedroom door and Francine was now scared and said that she didn't want to do it and at that time, Cindy kicked the door open. Francine was holding the gun at that time and it went off. She did say that Cindy never fired the gun and that she did not have a knife at that time.

"She said that her parents were in bed when Cindy kicked the door open and that her parents were sort of sleeping. Cindy had left shortly after the gun went off and Francine then followed Cindy out the front door. When asked, she said there was no one present at that time other than her and Cindy. She stated that she had thrown her clothes in the trash somewhere and that they, Cindy and Francine, had gone to Cindy's boyfriend's apartment to clean up and Randy, meaning the boyfriend, was asleep and they just washed off with wash rags.

"Frankie (Lieutenant Thrasher was the only officer to call her by this nickname) and Cindy had talked about doing this to Cindy's parents, too, she told me. She said that Cindy was having just about any problems that you could have with them, meaning her parents. Francine stated that the only problems that she was having with her parents was that she wanted to move out. She stated that the knife came from the kitchen, that she got the knife while Cindy was outside the house.

"She stated that she went back to the bedroom and that her mother was awake and Cindy was outside. She, Francine, had pulled the phones out of the walls in the house and that she met Cindy outside in the silver Chevrolet S10 pickup.

"I asked Francine if she would go with me to the place where they had thrown the gun in the lake and she indicated a reluctance to do so. At that time, I presented her with a map of the City of Stillwater and asked her if she would make an X on the map at the location where the gun was thrown and she did that."

"Did she make any further comments about the knife wounds on her parents?"

"Yes, sir, considerable comments."

"What comments were those?"

"Continuing with the interview, she stated that Cindy threw the gun in the water, as she, Francine, who was driving the truck slowed down. She said that she hadn't talked to the police earlier because she was scared and that the planning for the murders had taken place at Cindy's boyfriend's apartment and that it happened pretty much the way that they planned it, except they planned that one or two shots would have taken care of it.

"She indicated that there were extra clothes in Cindy's truck, clothes that belonged to Cindy, for her to put on. And at that time, we took a break from the interview and I left the room momentarily."

DA Anderson inquired about the exact time the interview resumed, and Bowyer repeated his objection to the testimony regarding the Miranda rights.

Lieutenant Thrasher repeated the statement by Francine that she just wanted to be free of her parents and that her parents had told her if she moved out she would lose her car and they would not help her with college.

Continuing that line of questioning, Thrasher stated, "Frankie ran outside the house. Cindy was already outside. This was after the shots were fired."

"What then?"

"Francine said that she remembered going to the kitchen and remembered that the knife was in a drawer."

Thrasher continued his report, "Francine said that the bedroom door was open when she went back to the bedroom. Her dad was laying on the bed. Her mother had gotten up and was standing up. When asked, Francine said that her mother neither came toward her or fought her. Francine's mother was between the bed and the dresser screaming and yelling when she was stabbed. Francine stated she stabbed her mother, but could not remember how many times. At this time, her mother did not fall down. She said that her mother went to the other side of the bed, and that she followed her mother."

Bowyer again objected to the testimony.

Continuing, Thrasher unemotional, and matter-of-factly stated, "Francine said that at this time, she again stabbed her mother and her mother fell down by the dresser, the dresser with the mirror. Francine said she left the room. She couldn't remember stabbing her father. According to her, Cindy was not there at the time. Cindy walked back into the house while Francine was in the bedroom and Francine saw her either in the bedroom or the hall. Francine said that she pulled the phone out of the wall in the bedroom at the time that her mother ran from the glass door side of the bed to the dresser with the mirror side of the bed. Francine again stated that she had stabbed her mother first by the glass doors in the bedroom. That her mother then ran to the other side of the bed or to the dresser side of the bed screaming and this was the time that she had pulled the phone from the wall. Francine said she stabbed her mother again by the dresser and her mother fell down."

"Your Honor, I again renew my objection as far as Miranda."

"It's in the record."

"You may continue."

"Francine said that the knife was still in her mother. Again she said that she did not remember stabbing her father. At this time, she ran from the bedroom. Cindy was in the living room. Francine said that she and Cindy placed the gun that was used in a duffel bag. Francine then went back and closed the bedroom door.

"Francine said that we, meaning her and Cindy, went out to the truck and left. She stated that she pulled the kitchen phone from the wall when she went into the house to get the knife. She stated that she went outside after the gun went off and then went back inside to get the knife. Francine stated that she and Cindy had kidded about doing this six or eight weeks ago at somebody's house. She stated that she never offered anybody any money to do it and that she never tried to buy any attachments for the gun. And at this time, it was eleven fifteen p.m. and the interview was concluded."

"What occurred to Ms. Stepp at the conclusion of the interview?"

"We accompanied her to the squad room of the Police Department. In that it was late at night, we ordered some food for her and her relatives."

"Let me withdraw that. Was she taken into custody at this time?"

"After a period of time, later that night, she was taken into custody."

Bowyer then renewed his objection and added that the State had used psychological coercion.

The Judge asked for quiet in the courtroom, and then said, "Go Ahead."

Bowyer spoke forcefully, "Psychological coercion, undue influence, the warnings were not read and followed precisely. At no time did this officer or any other officer ask my client if she could read. I believe the officer will testify when it comes to cross-examination on this point that as a reward for making comments to the police, the police department bought her a pizza!

"Further, that she was under undue influence from her family members who were present. And I will renew my motion to have this testimony stricken; that my client has been denied due process of law and requests at this time the case be dismissed."

Anderson replied, "In brief response, I would say the issue is not whether Ms. Stepp can read, but whether she can hear and the issue is not whether she can write, but whether she can talk. We would rest on that argument."

Bowyer couldn't resist adding, "Your Honor, I know you are going to give us a recess, but one last thing. In support of our motion, I don't think it has been made clear to the Court that in support of these oral motions at this point, there will be written motions forthcoming, to which the defense will supply the Court a tape, video tape furnished both defense Counsel as evidence in support of the Motion to Suppress and the psychological coercion that was involved and directed towards my client."

"All right. Very Good. We will recess."

After the brief recess, Anderson called Dennis McGrath to the stand, for the second time. He was handed State's Exhibit 54, the Adult Miranda Right form used by the police department. He identified Cindy Wynn's signature placed there. The time of the interview was after the Stepp interview.

Ms. Ramsey objected, and the Court noted it.

"Did she discuss her involvement in that homicide, if any?"

"Yes, sir, she did."

"What did she say?"

"At approximately midnight on the night of the homicide, both herself and Francine had returned to the house for Cindy to pick up some cigarettes and change that she had left on the kitchen counter. As they got back to the house, they both went inside and Cindy went to the counter to pick up the cigarettes and the change. When she turned around, Francine walked into the area where she was standing and had a gun. Cindy turned around and she tried to grab the gun from Francine's hand and asked, 'what the hell are you doing?' According to Cindy, Francine's response was, 'I'm tired of it and can't stand it no more' and then ran toward the bedroom.

"Cindy became scared, screamed and ran outside. She heard the gunshot and Francine came running back outside. When Francine came out, she saw that she had a knife in her hand and Cindy thought that Francine was going to kill her and then ran towards her parents' residence. Francine ran after her saying, 'I'm not going to kill you, I'm not going to kill you.'"

"Objection, Your Honor. Hearsay." Bowyer was on his feet.

The objection was sustained, and at Bowyer's request, the Judge ordered the hearsay testimony stricken from the record.

Anderson suggested that McGrath continue.

"My mom is not dead, what am I going to do? Cindy again..."

Bowyer objected again and it was sustained. The Court illuminated his instructions, "I'm only asking that the statements attributed to Stepp, not the statements that Wynn was saying herself."

Anderson said, "You may continue."

"Cindy asked, 'what are you doing' and screamed. Francine ran back into the house. When Francine came back outside, she told Cindy to get in the truck and even helped Cindy to get one of her feet into the truck and they drove to Boomer Lake. Cindy said that she didn't throw the gun in the lake, that Francine did. They went back to Cindy's house on High Point and washed off in the bathroom. When they got there, Randy Jackson was asleep and Cindy crawled in bed with him. According to Cindy, Francine went to sleep and Cindy stayed up for the remainder of the night. When the alarm went off, Francine was standing at the foot of Cindy's bed. Apparently Cindy had fallen asleep for a little bit. Francine then left.

"After further questioning, Cindy stated that she had kicked the door to the Stepp bedroom. When she saw the gun, she became scared, went to the door, turned the knob and tried to open it but it wouldn't open, so she kicked the door and at the time she kicked the door, the parents inside sat up in bed. The Mom pulled the covers up to her chest and at the same time Francine shot, she saw Francine's father go down and the mother yelled Francine's name. Cindy got scared and thought she was going to be shot and ran out of the house.

"After further questioning, Cindy replied that she didn't see anything else, ran out of the house and didn't see any of the stabbing. She stayed outside the house. She saw Francine come out of the house at one point with the knife, to which Cindy asked, 'What are you doing?' 'What are you doing?'"

The District Attorney asked him to continue.

"At the conclusion, she said that they went and the gun was thrown into Boomer Lake in a duffel type bag. They got out into the truck, Francine changed clothes in the truck, took her boots off and changed her pants. At that point, they drove to a laundromat and rinsed the clothes off. Francine's boots were dipped in a commode and the blood was rinsed off the boots. They threw the clothes away, got back in the truck and went back to Cindy's apartment on High Point."

At this point Ms. Ramsey asked, "Your Honor, I would request clarification as to whose clothes."

McGrath answered, "Francine's."

Ms. Ramsey replied, "Thank you."

That concluded McGrath's testimony. Both defense counsels reserved the right of cross-examination of the witness.

Ms. Ramsey stated, "Your Honor, we would have no objection to Mr. Anderson's recitation of the facts and we would also agree to that and would request we be in recess until the 26th, as far as Courtroom appearance is concerned, other than with the Motions to Suppress to be determined at a later time."

Judge Belden responded, "All right, at this time..."

Bowyer put in, "I would join in that motion, Your Honor, as far as the District Attorney's statements concerning filing of motions and such. We would, of course, contest all other statements made by the District Attorney."

The exhibits, drawings and diagrams of the Stepp residence, were placed in the custody of the Court Reporter.

Court was adjourned.

The testimony left many questions unanswered and many spectators feeling baffled and curious.

"What was her mother doing all the time Francine was running out of the house, talking to Cindy, getting a knife from the kitchen and going back to the bedroom?" One grey-haired woman asked her friend as they walked to their respective cars.

"Maybe the mother was too much in shock to try to do anything." The friend suggested.

"Of course, it would be a shock to wake up and see your only daughter with a weapon in her hand, firing at you, but still, as athletic as she was, you would have thought the mother could have gotten out of the house, or called somebody, or something!"

"Have you driven by the house where it happened? The houses set on large lots, so there's quite a bit of distance between them, but it does seem strange no one in the neighborhood heard anything."

The courtroom crowd eagerly awaited the answers to the many questions they felt would come out in the future trial.

Chapter Nine

The bane of every policeman's life is paperwork. From the earliest frontier marshalls who complained about the federal forms they were required to fill out to receive their expense accounts, to the modern day cops grousing about the stacks of paper they are required to process, that gripe remains the same.

The Incidental Report each officer is required to fill out is a standard form. There is a place for the complaint number, the beat or sector, date including exact time of day, nature of the incident, victim's name, date of birth, sex, home address and phone number. There are places for article name (if robbery) brand, model number, miscellaneous value, and the reporting officer's name.

Most of the page is blank ruled paper. The officers are instructed to keep their reports short and to the point. They write in summary style. Each report is reviewed and approved and it can be routed to the District Attorney, Criminal Investigation Department, City Attorney, Juvenile, etc. At the bottom right hand corner is a box marked Investigate Case Status with four boxes that may be checked: open, cleared, suspended, and unfounded.

Bartram was filling out one of these reports when he was interrupted by McGrath. He threw his Cross mechanical pencil down in disgust when the lead snapped. The paper work all seemed so pointless.

"What the hell do you want?"

The smile faded from McGrath's face as he recoiled from the anger in Bartram's. "Nothing," he mumbled, "Sorry I bothered you." He turned away but then swung back and asked innocently, "Your hemorrhoids in an uproar again?"

"There's nothing wrong with me except assholes that won't let me get this damn paperwork done." Bartram's tone of voice was softer this time.

The Stepp case appeared cleared by the arrest and subsequent conviction. There was nothing left for the police to do. They had arrested the perpetrators, testified at the hearings, and the job was over.

Sergeant Bartram did not experience the jubilation that he expected to feel at the end of a successful criminal investigation.

He brooded for a time, then picked up the phone and called a protestant minister. The Stillwater Police Department does not have a Chaplain, but it has members of the Ministerial Alliance who fill that function on a rotating basis. The police officers get to know them and the ministers realize they are providing a valuable service.

"I don't go to your church," Bartram spoke into the phone, "And I don't really plan to go to your church, but I need to talk with someone. Could you give me some of your time?"

The Reverend graciously agreed, and Bartram drove to the rectory, where they sat in the preacher's study.

After their initial greeting and chit-chat, he asked, "How may I help you? What seems to be troubling you?"

Bartram ran his fingers through his curly black hair in distraction, "I don't know what's the matter with me. I'm snapping at Dennis, that's McGrath, my partner, and we've always gotten along real good. I'm arguing with my wife all the time. Even my kids get on my nerves, when I'm home with them, which isn't that often. I find I'm yelling at them. My mother's not in good health, she has a heart condition, and I stalked off after a disagreement with her. I feel guilty as hell about that. What's the matter with me? I just feel like I want to be alone, just left totally alone. I can do my job, but that's it. I don't want anyone hassling me."

"Have you had a physical check-up lately?"

"Yeah, and the doctor says my cholesterol and blood pressure are too high. He wants me to start eating fish and stuff like that. I hate fish! Now I can't even enjoy a good steak dinner. My life is going down the toilet, Reverend."

"I've seen the way you work, Billy. I've ridden in the patrol car with you, and I'm familiar with the stress you policemen are under. My advice would be to be kinder to yourself, and you will discover that you can then be kinder to others. I think you need some time off from work."

"But I like my work! I like the evidence collection at the crime scene. I even like working dead bodies. I know it sounds crazy. There are some men who would rather do anything than work a dead body, but to me it's like a giant puzzle. The victims can't tell you anything. It is up to me to figure out what really happened to them. You have to be so careful collecting evidence! The more I throw myself into my work, the more I forget the problems at home. But I can only work sixteen hour days so long. I tell you something, some nights I have slept on the floor of the office rather than go home."

The minister looked grave. "I think you are suffering from a six letter word. It's called stress." He held up his hand, as Billy started to speak, "No, hear me out. I've talked with other police officers and I am aware of the statistics. Three out of four police marriages will end in divorce. I think it is due in part to the stress of their jobs.

"Our bodies are made for fight or flight. When the adrenalin starts pumping, we are ready to take action. You are forced, by your occupation to deny those feelings. You must make critical, life threatening decisions, in the fraction of a minute. All of these things are stressful."

"But I like my work!" Bartram protested.

"It's commendable that you like your work, but let me show you something." The Reverend drew a circle on a piece of paper. "You see this big circle is labeled work. These smaller ones are family, friends, hobbies, and church." At the frown on Bartram's face, he elaborated, "I didn't say my church, I just said church, any church. Now if your circle becomes too distorted, say the work circle takes up all the other space so there is nothing left for family, friends, and hobbies, you become 'out of round'. Are you following me?"

He turned the paper toward Bartram showing him a circle composed entirely of work, with tiny little circles for the other components of life.

"Tell yourself when you leave Police Headquarters, that you are closing the door on it. You are going to forget about it entirely. You are going to concentrate on the other important aspects of your life. There's a good message in that old song, *Stop and Smell the Roses*."

Bartram looked a little disappointed in the man's lecture. He had hoped for something more concrete. He still felt bruised and irritable inside, and an uneasy dejection that he could not name.

The minister was aware that the counseling session was not over. He shrewdly asked the sergeant about his work, and the past few months of work came tumbling out. He listened carefully as Bartram described the frantic pace of the last few months.

Gently, the preacher asked, "When your wife was having babies, did you ever read about Post Partum Depression?"

Bartram nodded, confused. What did that have to do with what they were talking about?

"I am acquainted with several people who have written books, designed a building, painted a large mural, and they agree. Completion of a major project can cause a person to feel depressed and let down and irritable. The project that took all their time, all their waking moments, all their energies is finished. There is nowhere else to go, nothing quite so compelling or interesting to take its place. I believe, in addition to stress, that also is your problem."

Slowly, Bartram admitted, "The Stepp case bothers me a lot. I have seen only one bloodier murder in my years on the force. I guess the thing that bothers me so much is that Francine and Cindy appear so normal. We deal with low lives all the time. An old ex-con has an alcoholic wife, and their kids are stealing and drinking and getting thrown in jail from the time they can walk. Well, you can kind of expect it. What chance did those little tykes have anyway? But Francine is different. Her folks cared for her, provided for her, were just normal people. How could she do that to them? It shook me. I'll confess it did."

The pastor agreed. "It would shake anyone." He paused for a moment and then said, "My favorite book of the Bible is the book of Job. I like to read it and just sit still awhile and think on it. Here was this man, this very good man, with everything taken away. His neighbors are patronizing him, scolding him, insinuating he brought his troubles on himself. It's a great scripture lesson to read that and ponder on it."

"I'm not too much for reading the Bible, or going to church," Bartram admitted. "I know they are good things to do, but it seems like I never have time."

The minister said, "I understand. I hope you will try to balance your life more. You don't want a divorce. I know you love your wife and children. Try to shut the door on police work when you leave Headquarters. Think of it as one little compartment in your brain. When you walk out the door, you close the door to that compartment. I think if you give yourself permission to enjoy the small things in life, the hug of a wife, the laugh of a child, the warmth of a good friend, you will find you are much happier!"

Bartram continued seeing the pastor a few more times for counseling sessions and advice.

McGrath knew the worst was over and Bartram was getting back to normal the evening Bartram came into the station, grinning.

"You'll never believe what happened just now."

McGrath said, "Okay. I'll bite. What happened?"

"Well, I was out on Country Club road, following this big Caddie that seemed to have a hard time keeping in his lane. The old guy wasn't driving very fast and I was debating if I should pull him over for a sobriety check when we get to the corner, and he just zooms across the intersection, veers to the right, jumps the bar ditch and lands in the pasture."

A little crowd of cops gathered, listening. "Well, I'm so astounded for a minute I just sit there. Then, while I'm wondering if he's all right, or if I should call for an ambulance, I observe him getting out of the car, and walking back to my patrol car, very carefully. He gets back to my car, leans over and says, 'I'm afraid I'll have to see your license.'"

The crowd snickered. McGrath was chuckling, "He's asking you for *your* license?"

Bartram nods, smiling, "I started laughing, I couldn't help it. He stares at me kind of sad and says, 'I screwed up, didn't I?'"

The group of cops dispersed and McGrath slapped Bartram on the shoulders. It was almost like old times, back before the Stepp murders, when they could smile and laugh about the crazy aspects of their jobs.

Chapter Ten

The fifth day of October, 1988, was another Indian summer day, pleasantly warm after the searing days of Oklahoma's hottest summer in fifty years. The crowd that gathered in the Payne County Courthouse were impatient to hear more about the Stepp murders. Every seat was taken in the courtroom.

After the Court announced, "This afternoon the Case of the State of Oklahoma versus Francine Marie Stepp," the District Attorney, Paul Anderson stated that the State was present and ready.

Anderson, a large man with an amiable face towered over defense counsel, Jack Bowyer, a short, stocky built man with the shoulders of an athlete. Bowyer responded, "Defendant Stepp is present and ready, Your Honor."

The defendant sat with her head bowed, her arms crossed in front of her chest.

Attorney Cheryl Ramsey stated, "Defendant Wynn is present and ready."

Defendant Cindy Wynn was alert, tilting her head from one side to the other and occasionally looking over her shoulder at the spectators in the courtroom.

The District Attorney read that the State was eager to

proceed at the earliest case charging Francine Stepp of murder in the first degree, counts one and two.

Francine, eighteen years old, appeared very slender and frail looking, wearing a plain blouse and straight skirt that covered her knees. She kept her head bowed, her eyes fixed on the floor. Her bright red hair was cut short and she appeared to be wearing very little makeup. She continued to hug herself as if she were cold.

Hardly had he finished speaking when Bowyer said, "After very lengthy discussions with my client and hours of discussing what a preliminary hearing is, that the burden is on the State to show that there's probable cause to believe that a crime was committed and to believe my client committed it, at this time Your Honor, my client chooses to waive her right to any further preliminary hearing in this matter."

The Judge then asked Francine if she was satisfied with the discussions she'd had about preliminary examination with her attorney, and if she had any questions. He continued to question her thoroughly in her understanding. Finally, Bowyer asked, "Your Honor, we are requesting to be bound over instanter."

"Very well."

And then Bowyer threw the bombshell that shocked the waiting spectators. He stated that after very lengthy discussions and hours of conversing with his client, she requested she would waiver her right to jury trial, waive her right to a non-jury trial and enter a plea of guilty to the charge, based solely on the plea negotiations with the District Attorney's office.

There was a hushed silence in the courtroom as people strained to hear what was being said. Surely, there was some mistake, it sounded like her lawyer was saying that she was going to plead guilty to the charges.

Judge Worthington, peered over his horn-rimmed glasses and asked Francine her name and age. She replied quietly that she was eighteen. He asked if she would like the information about the proceedings read to her and if she was taking any medications at this time. Then he asked if she had a history of emotional or mental illness, to which she replied in the negative. He asked if she was under the influence of drugs or alcohol at this time and again she answered no. He asked if she had discussed the proceedings with her attorney to her satisfaction and she answered yes.

Then the Judge asked Bowyer, "What can you tell me of your client's competency?"

"Your Honor, concerning my client's competency, I've had approximately one hundred fifty hours of personal contact with my client. I would state to the court that on every contact that I have had with my client, she has rationally and intelligently responded to the questions that I have posed to her. And as indicated on my certificate of counsel, Your Honor, it's my impression that she is competent to proceed; and she's also competent to understand the consequences of entering a plea in this regard. And I would state to the court that after long discussions with my client, I believe that she is freely and voluntarily doing this, Your Honor. She's under no threats or coercion of any kind."

Then the Judge asked Francine if the signature on the document before him was her signature and she responded that it was.

Judge Worthington carefully went over her certain guaranteed constitutional rights under the Justice system.

He told her that she had a right to a trial by jury and she stated that she understood that. He continued, "You have a right to face, confront witnesses that appear against you, and to have your attorney cross-examine them. Do you realize you have that right?"

"Under our system you also have the right against self incrimination. that simply means that you have a right to remain silent, if you wish to do so. And the District Attorney nor anyone else could comment about your silence before a jury hearing the case. Do you realize that you have that?"

Again she answered, "Yes."

He continued, "And that further means that you could not be compelled to testify against yourself. Did you discuss that with Mr. Bowyer and know that you have all of these rights?"

Quietly, Francine answered, "Yes."

"You also have the right to have witnesses appear in court in your behalf. And the court would compel their attendance, if you asked it to. Do you know that?"

"Yes."

"And under our system of justice and the law, you are presumed innocent of these charges against you. And this presumption remains with you at all times until and unless the State would prove your guilt beyond a reasonable doubt to the satisfaction of a jury or judge hearing the case. Do you know that presumption of innocence is yours?"

"Yes."

"Did you discuss with Mr. Bowyer and do you fully understand that when you enter a plea of guilty, you give up all these rights and the presumption of innocence?"

"Yes."

"And you tell me that you wish to do that?"

"Yes."

"Are you or has anyone close to you been threatened or pressured or coerced for you to enter a plea of guilty to this charge?"

"No."

"You assure me and tell me that this is your own choosing?"

"Yes."

"Do you know what the penalties provided by law are for the crime of Murder in the First Degree?"

"Yes."

"Would you tell me please what you understand that to be?"

"Maximum of death and minimum of life in prison."

"Then tell me please why you plead guilty to Count One, the charge of Murder in the First Degree of Mark Stanley Stepp?"

"Because I took the life of my father."

This was repeated again concerning the murder of Delores June Stepp, and she responded that she took the life of her mother.

Judge Worthington asked, "And again you actually did what the State accuses you of doing?"

"Yes."

"Then please tell me how do you plead?" He repeated the charges and the names of the deceased and she answered Guilty to each.

Anderson then spoke up, "Your Honor, I am authorized to tell the Court that each and every member of the surviving family of Mark and Delores Stepp urges the Court to impose a sentence of life, that the defendant be incarcerated in the penitentiary for the rest of her natural life. Based on her age and notwithstanding the facts and circumstances of this offense, I do believe that recommendation is appropriate. The State of Oklahoma also makes that recommendation in each count, with the further recommendation that these two terms be served concurrently."

Bowyer added, "That is our understanding of the recommendation, Your Honor."

The Judge addressed the solemn, white-faced young woman standing before him, "Miss Stepp, do you have anything to say before I impose judgement and sentence?"

So softly that those in front barely heard, she responded, "No, sir."

Then the Judge accepted her plea and as punishment sentenced her to serve a term of life on each count. He advised her that she had a right to appeal this judgment and sentence to the Court of Criminal Appeals, and if she could not afford the services of an attorney the court would appoint an attorney to represent her. She was then remanded to the custody of the Sheriff.

There was a general stirring and restlessness on the part of the spectators in the courtroom. It was over! Francine had pled guilty and been sentenced. The "facts and circumstances of this offense" that had been mentioned, remained in the realm of speculation. A lot of people were simply stunned. They had expected Francine to reveal what had precipitated her violent actions, and she accepted her sentence as she had accepted the witnesses at the hearing, with total silence.

Then Anderson spoke firmly, "The State next calls the case of the State of Oklahoma versus Cindy Sue Wynn,

Counts One and Two, alleging conspiracy to commit murder in the first degree and accessory after the fact."

Defense counsel Ramsey then stood and advised the court that Cindy Wynn waived formal reading of the information in both cases and that they had completed a petition to enter a plea of guilty, a motion for the accountability plan under the Youthful Offender's Act and a waiver of the ten day waiting period. Ms. Ramsey asked and received permission to approach the bench. While her attorney and the Judge were conferring, Cindy was seated at the table. Cindy's eyes danced in her heart-shaped face. Her blonde hair showed some dark roots, but she was dressed as conservatively as Francine. She reached over, took a yellow sheet of legal size paper that Ms. Ramsey kept for her use, and using her lawyer's pen, printed on it in big letters: TEN YEARS. She turned around to the court spectators and mouthed at them, "And I'll never serve a day."

Unaware of the scene played out behind her, Ms. Ramsey then said, "At this time Miss Wynn wishes to enter a plea of guilty to the charge of Accessory, Counts One and Two and to Conspiracy, Counts One and Two. And I believe Miss Wynn is ready to proceed at this time."

The Judge then asked Cindy if she understood and agreed with those statements and she answered yes. He inquired if she was taking any medication at that time, to which the reply was no. He asked Ms. Ramsey about her client's competency and after being assured of that, he questioned Cindy about the documents that she had initialed. He explained again, as he had to Francine, about her constitutional rights, and the presumption of innocence. Then he asked if she knew the possible penalty for each of the counts of conspiracy to commit murder.

When she replied in affirmative, he asked her what she understood that penalty to be.

Cindy's voice was audible in the courtroom, "Conspiracy, maximum of ten years and a five thousand dollar fine."

"And do you know what the punishment provided by law is for each of the counts of accessory after the fact?"

"Yes, Your Honor."

"Tell me what you understand that to be."

"A maximum of five years, and a five hundred dollar fine."

"Knowing all these rights that you have and knowing that by entering a plea of guilty you surrender and give them up, and knowing what the penalties provided by law are for these offenses, do you tell me that you still wish to plead guilty?"

"Yes, Your Honor."

"And tell me why?"

"Because I was inside the Stepp residence and I ran outside."

"Pardon me?"

"I was inside the Stepp residence and then I ran outside."

"You're going to have to do better than that."

"At the time of the crime, I was inside the Stepp residence. And right before it actually began and finished I was outside the Stepp residence."

The Judge solemnly informed her, "You're charged with aiding and assisting Francine Marie Stepp after the commission of murder in the first degree."

"Okay, the police officers have two witnesses saying that, the testimony was that I was at their house planning to commit this crime. And I helped her dispose of her clothes."

"Now, are you quoting somebody else, or are you telling me what you did?"

"No, I did aid her in disposing of the clothes."

"Are you telling me that you actually did what the State accuses you of having done in these cases?"

"Yes, Your Honor."

Then followed the reading of the four charges and Cindy Wynn pled guilty four times.

"The Court will accept the plea of guilty of the defendant. And will delay pronouncement of judgement and sentence until February 22, 1989 at one thirty p.m. And by reason of her age, the defendant is ordered to the delayed sentencing program for young adults of the Department of Corrections of the State of Oklahoma with confinement. The Department of Corrections is ordered to prepare a specialized offender accountability plan for this defendant and to file it with the Court with a copy to the District Attorney and a copy to defense counsel at least twenty days prior to the date set for sentencing as provided by law."

After her attorney ascertained that the proper writs would be prepared, the Court was recessed.

The spectators filed out the double doors, talking to each other and buzzing with rumors.

While the crowd was speculating, two of the lawmen who investigated the case were walking down the steps of the courthouse quietly.

Both Lieutenant Ron Thrasher and Sergeant Billy Bartram were silent. As they got into the police car to return to the station, Thrasher sighed, "It's been a long, hot summer!"

Bartram nodded, agreeing, "That it has."

Behind them on the steps the courtroom watchers agreed that it was a shame the case hadn't come before a jury where all the facts of the case could have been brought out.

Chapter Eleven

Two women sit on death row at Mabel Bassett Correctional Center, the only maximum security facility for women in the state of Oklahoma. The state has abolished the electric chair in McAlister Penitentiary, in favor of the more humane lethal injection. Sources close to Francine Stepp say that one reason she pled guilty was because she feared a jury might sentence her to death.

On Martin Luther King Blvd, in Oklahoma City, next to the old brick building that houses Department of Corrections offices is the parking lot and double chain link fences with razor wire on top and video cameras at intervals.

A sign reads: YOU MUST REMAIN 15 FEET FROM FENCE AT ALL TIMES. Another sign at the entrance double gates reads: ALL PERSONS ENTERING INSTALLATION ARE SUBJECT TO SEARCH. The department of corrections officials take security very seriously, indeed.

A big metal building houses the gymnasium, where basketball games are played. There are exercise bicycles, weight lifting machines, two pool tables, vending machines for candy and soft drinks, and large roll-around toys are stored here for visiting days. Visitors are permitted in the gymnasium on visiting days. While most visitors are subject only to "pat searches", inmates are strip-searched after visitors leave, and may be cavity searched, if the officials deem it necessary.

Many of the residents of Mabel Bassett have children, and the toughest part of the visiting days is the heart-rending scenes of little children being forcibly removed from their mothers' arms. The Assistant Warden, Pat Lloyd, a very personable young woman with a kindly manner, says it sometimes takes a few days for the mothers to settle down after such a visit.

Oklahoma has one of the highest incarceration rates of any state in the union. Oklahoma ranks forty-sixth in money spent on education, but the Department of Corrections, surprisingly, is very progressive and forward-thinking in their handling of female offenders. They do not refer to the women in Mabel Bassett as female offenders. They are called "ladies" and "residents". A small matter, perhaps, but one that appears to be very astute. Just as in allowing the women to wear blue jeans and blouses, rather than uniforms, it creates a more pleasant atmosphere than most prisons, and is designed to get the residents' cooperation.

There are smaller metal buildings that house the educational areas. There is a horticulture department— all the grounds are kept up by the residents. There are education buildings for 2nd through 6th grade, and 7th through 12th grade. All residents leave with a General Education Diploma, and some arrive almost totally illiterate. A talk-back television program allows residents to earn an Associate's Degree.

Residents who are shortly to be released live in three areas on the second and third floors of the Department of

Corrections. There are no bars or partitions, only waist high walls to divide the cubicles where cots and metal storage cabinets hold the personal belongings of the residents. Large mirrors are evident, as are ironing boards and hair curlers, as these residents, often on work release projects, get ready to resume their places in the outside world.

The young women who walk the pathways between buildings, or sun themselves (strict rules govern how much skin they may expose) beside the buildings, look like the proverbial "girl next door". There are no grossly deformed, extremely ugly individuals. On the contrary, compared to a cross-section of the general population, they would probably rank better than average-looking.

The medium security building is west of the maximum security, and the women can be seen walking to class, hanging out clothes (there is a laundry, but some women prefer to wash out their own clothes by hand in the plastic bucket provided each resident.)

The residents earn $12 per month. They may purchase items, such as shampoo, toothpaste, etc. at the canteen. There is a beauty shop, staffed by residents. No bartering between the residents is a rule the officials try to enforce. Bartering can lead to serious acts of misconduct, but it would appear the instinct of humans to barter items is a hard one to suppress.

The maximum security section of the building's quadrant is a pressed type concrete construction with razor wire on top. Inside, the walls and doors are electronically controlled from a main control room that resembles a submarine's central control room. Every door is electronically controlled and none open until another is closed. No bars are visible, but polished wire glass separates each of the four main parts of the building. The officer in control monitors TV screens that reveal each section.

Each discipline unit has a white door with a slot near the bottom, called the "bean hole" where food is passed to the inmate. For offenses, such as being violent, assaulting others, or attempting escape, the resident may be kept in disciplinary unit, being removed only one hour out of twenty four hours for exercise. They are allowed two showers a week.

The residents of the maximum security section are brought out for exercise in handcuffs. After they are inside the chain link exercise yard, they put their hands out through a hole in the gate, for the handcuffs to be taken off. When it's time to return the process is repeated. Maximum security residents are marched together by guards to the eating hall, where they have fifteen minutes to eat.

Residents are awakened at five thirty a.m. There are two showers for forty-two women. By eight fifteen a.m., all forty-two residents of a quadrangle have to be showered, dressed, all curlers out of hair and beds made up. Television sets are permitted in the individual cells, if the resident earns good behavior points to have them. Each Quadrant, in the "day room" or sitting room has a big color TV and the center has all the cable channels, except for the movie channels. The most popular channel is MTV, the rock music channel.

Residents have an organization formed in 1982, called Prison Prevention, Speak Out Program. Residents are not given any credits or privileges for their participation in the program, but it is popular, nonetheless. As school age children often tour the facility, the women speak to the groups in the conference room of the Corrections headquarters. They hope to prevent youths from making wrong choices and getting behind bars.

At the present time, neither Francine nor Cindy are participating in these speak out programs, but Francine is a model prisoner.

Francine looks better now in Mabel Bassett than at any time since she was arrested. Her eyes are clear, her complexion smooth, her figure filled out with the twenty pounds she's added with the starchy prison food. She keeps to herself, has progressed from working in the laundry to working in the industrial building, and plans to get her Associate's Degree.

Cindy Wynn's blonde hair has grown out brown now. Cindy has actually lost weight on the prison diet and her cheekbones are now visible in her face. Ironically, she too, looks better than when she was arraigned. Cindy had some trouble adjusting to prison life, even though she was put in minimum security when she arrived at Mabel Bassett Correctional Center, unlike Francine, who was put in maximum security. Cindy's propensity for making smart remarks has not endeared her to the officials, although her quick wit makes it easy for her to get laughs from her fellow residents.

Both Francine and Cindy have declined interviews on the advice of their attorneys. They would like to resume their lives after parole as anonymously as possible. Oklahoma is one of three states that has open parole notices published in newspapers so that victims and their families may present their objections or recommendations.

Chapter Twelve

Judge Donald L. Worthington is a tall, grey haired man, who puts on horn-rimmed glasses to read, reminding one of the actor Jimmy Stewart, in appearance, if not in voice. He is known as a patient man, courteous, not given to angry outbursts, but not willing to suffer foolishness, either.

In an empty courtroom, on February 22, 1989, two Correction officers led Cindy Wynn, in handcuffs, waist chains and ankle chains (they were removed before the crowd gathered in the courtroom). Both women officers wore the dark jackets, brown pants and white shirts with Department Of Corrections emblems on them. They were armed. One stood near the door while the other sat in the jury box.

Cindy Wynn wore a turquoise colored sweat shirt, blue jeans and bright yellow tennis shoes. Her large expressive eyes were emphasized by blue eye shadow. Her attorney, Cheryl Ramsey, was neatly attired as usual in a dark suit, white blouse and black pumps.

The court was called to order, and Cindy and her attorney stood in front of the judge's bench for sentencing.

"Do you recall your previous plea of guilty in the court?"

"Yes, sir."

"Do you have any questions?"

"No, sir."

"The Court having previously accepted your plea of guilty, finds you guilty as charged. On count one accessory after the fact, you are hereby sentenced to serve five years, to be served concurrently. On count one accessory to conspiracy to commit murder, you are hereby sentenced to serve ten years. On count two accessory after the fact, you are hereby sentenced to serve five years, to be served concurrently. On count two accessory to conspiracy to commit murder, you are hereby sentenced to serve ten years."

As Judge Worthington spoke the first words, "You are sentenced to five years," Cindy started crying. She continued crying during the sentencing, and the bailiff got a yellow box of Kleenex and handed it to Cindy's attorney, who tried to give it to Cindy. She continued wiping her eyes with her hands, then folded her hands behind her, declining the tissues.

The Judge solemnly continued speaking, explaining that she had the right to an appeal and if she could not afford an attorney for the appeal an attorney would be appointed for her.

He denied a request by her attorney to allow her credit for the ninety-eight days she had spent in the Payne County Jail and the time she had been under the jurisdiction of the Department of Corrections, since October 18.

After court was adjourned, District Attorney Anderson gave a quote to the *Stillwater News Press*.

"I had serious reservations whether we could have proved Miss Wynn guilty beyond a reasonable doubt. There are only four people who know for a fact what occurred in the Stepp home that evening. Two of those people are dead and we are left with the statements of the other two. Francine said repeatedly that Cindy didn't assist her in the murder of her parents."

He explained to the reporters that most people who expressed a doubt that one girl could kill two people with a knife, unassisted by another person, were unaware of the medical examiner's testimony. That testimony indicated one of the gunshots first fired into the room lodged against Mark Stepp's spine, which in all probability completely immobilized him. "The pattern of the stab wounds also indicated he was defenseless and unable to resist. Conversely, Delores Stepp was stabbed repeatedly front to back while she was trying to resist Francine.

"Without question, Ms. Wynn was a major influence on Francine in the planning stages. She abandoned the plan but Francine carried it through."

He added that Ms. Wynn provided a continual alibi for Ms. Stepp for the period of the investigation until she finally gave her story to police officers. He noted that Ms. Wynn's voluntary confession to police officers was given only after she was aware that Ms. Stepp had provided a confession to the police.

"Obviously, we told Wynn's counsel what our recommendations would be and she admonished her not to discuss this and to conduct herself properly in the courtroom. Her disregard of her attorney's advice and making a sign with the figure "10" on it and showing it to supporters in the courtroom the day she entered the plea was typical and a great disappointment to all of us.

"For these and other reasons we have recommended the maximum punishment allowable by law for these offenses—we feel she is truly deserving of the sentence imposed by the court."

Cindy Wynn would have several long years to regret her rash disregard of proper courtroom propriety. If she thought the psychologists at Lexington would be easy to manipulate, she learned otherwise.

At the end of Cindy's first two years, she applied for parole. Parole was denied. She will undoubtedly apply again each year until she is eligible. Francine will not be eligible for parole for fifteen more years.

Chapter Thirteen

Almost every newspaper account of the Stepp case, from the initial discovery of the bodies, until the final sentencing of Cindy Wynn, also mentions the fact that Mark and Delores Stepp were nudists. They spent the last weekend of their lives at a nudist camp.

The *Wichita Eagle Beacon* newspaper ran a feature article in August, 1988 about the Sandy Lane Nudist Camp, where Mark and Dee Stepp were members.

Sex, perversion, mate swapping, loads of suggestive winking and leering—those are some of the images people conjure up about what goes on, but the women and men who participate maintain that it just doesn't happen.

Sandy Lane was started in 1957 by a few couples who were willing to drive down a bumpy, cedar lined road to a rustic camp. Through the members own participation and cooperative effort a swimming pool was built. By 1980 it had grown to over one hundred members, and was even the setting for a wedding *au naturel*. Sandy Lane has sixteen written rules, ranging from disposing of trash to prohibiting public displays of affection. They also have an unwritten rule to keep the attendance in balance between men and women. A single may join, but must bring a mate to belong, according to the anonymous spokesperson for the camp. "This helps keep the weirdos at bay." This policy is also different from other camps, where there is no effort at keeping an equal number of the sexes. One thing some other owners require is that if the person joining is married, they must bring their spouse, even if the spouse does not choose to disrobe—thus preventing people from coming to the ranch simply to meet a sexual partner.

Francine was a regular member of the First Methodist Sunday School and Youth group, and listened as the lessons of modesty were taught. How perplexed and bewildered must she have been at the contradictory advice she was getting? This element of her life, "One of our families' secrets that we don't tell anyone else," may have played a big part in Francine's awkwardness and withdrawal and her inability to confide in her school age companions.

One has to ask: How much hostility would be generated by parents taking a shy, sensitive girl to nudist camps, where she was expected to strip off her clothes and join the other children in activities? And how much did Francine resent these summer trips and outings?

After the newspaper printed the fact that she and her parents attended the nudist camp in Kansas, Francine told her boyfriend that she did not take her clothes off.

Teenagers develop special attire (follow fads) to distinguish themselves from adults and others who do not share their ideas, beliefs and practices.

Boots are seen as symbols of strength and when worn constantly, experts tell us the wearer is trying to give an impression of authority. In Francine's case, the wearing of boots would seem to indicate that in this one small area of her life, she was in charge. She was the wielder of power.

Delores Stepp was concerned with job advancement and happy over her promotion. Yet Dee usually wore navy or brown polyester slacks, unremarkable blouses and lace-up thick soled "earth" shoes. In an office where over a half dozen women work, some of whom skip lunch to indulge their fashion tastes, it appeared that her fashion statement was very plain, to deliberately dowdy.

Delores was very concerned with her figure, however. It is not surprising that she was one of the more than 180,000 women who had breast augmentation surgery.

Youth is IN, old age is OUT. There has probably never been generations of Americans more obsessed with youth than today. It is acceptable to have white hair and talk about your advanced age, as long as your face is unlined and your body trim.

At forty-one, Delores was not getting older, but better. She exercised regularly, lifting weights with Mark. She enjoyed sports, camping out and especially softball games.

Mark was a natural athlete, with grace and balance. He pitched, hit and ran with easy smoothness. If he was concerned with aging, it did not show. He was an active, outdoor loving man, not much given to introspection. There was no hint of another woman in his life. He seemed totally devoted to his wife and proud of their daughter.

Mark had more friends than Delores. Delores seemed to feel more at home with men than women. Women sometimes cried at her sharp remarks, while Mark's friends often found them hilariously funny.

Delores liked a ribald joke and could tell them without a blush to a mixed group. She and Mark were frankly sensual people who enjoyed their bodies and each other. They were just one of millions of couples who enjoy watching pornography and filming themselves in the nude. If there was ever jealousy between the two, no one seems to have known of it or remembers it.

They spent money on their daughter that they could have enjoyed spending on themselves. They bought her contacts when she asked for them. They had her teeth repaired by an orthodontist (no little expense) and they furnished her with clothes, toys and later an automobile, so that she would fit in with her crowd of peers.

Both Delores and Mark were people who lived on the surface of life. They never seemed to look beneath the obvious. Francine complied to their rules, therefore she must be happy. They never seemed to look for any signs that their daughter was unhappy. Why should she be unhappy? They provided an All-American home with all the comforts and conveniences of other families of similar income.

It is unsettling to many couples who are busily engaged in providing the creature comforts for their families to wonder if there is something lacking in their lives. Better to keep so busy with activities that there is no time to question or think about troubling issues. It was seldom that Francine dared cross them or question the commands of her parents. In that totally controlled atmosphere was breeding a fertile field of growing hatreds.

To argue about a parental order was to bring the parental wrath down on her head. Francine was a timid girl and did not often dare to challenge her parents. It was not until Francine observed the outrageous remarks and daring stunts that Cindy Wynn performed that she even realized rebellion was possible.

In a limited way, Francine was beginning to develop the longing to separate herself from her parents that comes to most teenagers earlier in life. In some ways she and Cindy both appear to have an intense longing for approval and attention.

Delores, self-confident and outgoing, could no more imagine how her daughter felt inside than an enthusiastic mountain climber who relishes the danger and exhilaration can imagine how a person suffering from a phobia of heights feels.

Off work, at the softball games that played such a big part in their lives, Dee's favorite attire was cutoff jean shorts, very tight and very short. Susan Turner, a friend of the family, remembers scolding Dee good-naturedly, "Girl, if you don't get some longer shorts, you're going to have another set of cheeks to powder!"

The teasing didn't phase Dee, she continued to wear her shorts. No one was going to dictate to her how to dress.

Susan Turner recalls one August evening at a softball game, Francine came out to the stands wearing tight blue jean shorts, heavy blue eye shadow, exactly like the eye shadow her mother affected, and a cigarette dangling from her mouth. She had never seen Francine smoke before and the attempt to mimic her mother was so obvious at first Susan didn't know what to say, then she decided to kid Francine. "Girl, you're going to have to get longer shorts or..."

Francine whirled around and snapped, "I'm eighteen years old and I'll wear what I please." (Actually, she wouldn't celebrate her eighteenth birthday until that December.) Several people standing around who overheard the exchange were surprised at the anger Francine displayed. She had always been such a meek, mild girl it seemed totally out of character for her to respond that way.

Francine's manner of dressing at school, the neon-colored sweaters in bright green or pink, along with the tight blue jeans and high heeled boots, combined with the punk-rock hair style seem at odds with what we know of her personality.

Teen years are a particularly difficult time in a youngster's life. If the teen is on the fringes of the popular, "in" crowd, unable or unwilling to follow the stylish fads, the youth may choose to be rebellious and pretend to care less about popularity.

Today's culture, with rock videos, horror movies, slasher films and heavy metal rock music that glorifies violence, suicide and death undoubtedly has an effect on teenagers.

Sean Sellers was sixteen years old when he shot and killed his mother and stepfather near Oklahoma City. This case was much publicized in Oklahoma, where Sellers was declared an adult, stood trial and was sentenced to death.

Sellers admitted he had been involved in Satanism since he was fourteen and had committed a previous murder of a convenience store clerk, "just to see how it felt to kill somebody."

It is ironic that neither Francine nor Cindy apparently knew very much about the Sellers case. He told a friend of his plans, and after killing his parents he was the one who "found" their bodies. It took the police just two days to put together the facts that Sean Sellers killed his parents.

Had they studied his mistakes, perhaps they would have been more successful at eluding arrest. One thing that strikes the reader of true police cases is how often the investigator senses that something is not right. No matter how a person tries to pretend grief and act the part of the bereaved person, the experienced investigator quite often detects the false act.

While it is true there are great differences in how people react to the shocking news of murder, still there are samenesses that have the ring of truth to the experienced investigator. Probably more individuals who have murdered their husbands or wives have been tripped up by police digging deeper, because "It just didn't feel right."

An especially tragic case of family members killed by a youth who was a teenage Satanist was that of Thomas Sullivan in New Jersey. He killed his mother and sibling and then committed suicide.

Satanists are overwhelmingly teenage boys. That may be because boys tend to be more attracted to fantasies of violence and power than are girls, according to Esther Davidowitz, author of articles on Satanism. She reports that teens may be especially vulnerable to Satanism's bizarre message that magic powers can be obtained through a kinship with the devil. Plus the Satanic cult's glorification of evil, destruction and instant gratification also offers rebellious teens a surefire way to shock their parents.

While there is no evidence that either Francine or Cindy were involved in Satanism, it is interesting that both mothers slain in Satanic murders, Thomas Sullivan's and Sean Sellers, were described as meticulous and strict.

The police did not find any books on Satanism in the Stepps' home. One friend of both Francine and Cindy, Jeff Adams, is admittedly into Satanism. He talks about it and likes to draw pictures of people being stabbed to death. He was questioned by the police and cleared of any involvement in the crime, but there are still people who wonder what influence he might have had.

Chapter Fourteen

Had Mark and Delores Stepp lived another three months and two weeks they would have celebrated their twentieth wedding anniversary. They married in September of 1968, a year that was marked by many bloody and violent acts, just as their own deaths were.

Martin Luther King, Jr. was gunned down in April of that year. Robert Kennedy was slain in June and half way around the world in Vietnam the tiny village of My Lai was bathed in blood.

No thoughts of death and violence marred the lovers' dreams and plans that summer. The Mammas and Pappas rock group and the Beatles' latest songs from the *Yellow Submarine* were heard at the bars in Newport they frequented. *Rosemary's Baby*, the chilling tale starring Mia Farrow, Barbara Streisand in *Funny Girl*, and *The Boston Strangler* were movies playing down the street.

Newport, Rhode Island was a heady place for Delores and Mark to be. From their small town backgrounds in conservative rural states to the elegant, freewheeling port city that frankly welcomes sailors with a row of taverns, pubs and saloons that line Harbor street. It was quite a contrast. During their time in the Navy Mark and Delores began the practices that were to figure so much in their later lives. Off the Naval Base, it was customary to head for the bars where everyone played shuffleboard, drank beer and sat around, talked and flirted. In the barracks, they became accustomed to nudity so that later the idea of joining a nudist camp was attractive to them.

Francine was born fourteen months after they married. A close friend discloses they had planned to name the baby Frank if it were a boy. She was a frail baby, and suffered from colds a lot her first two years.

The couple lived in Fond Du Lac, Wisconsin then, near Lake Winnebago. Mark found work at the big Mercury Marine plant there, and they enjoyed weekends at the lake. Dee also worked at Mercury, but in a different plant.

A man that worked with Dee for four years, recalls that he never knew Francine's name. Dee talked about her daughter a great deal, but her co-worker insists he did not know if the child was a boy or girl, since the constant reference was "the kid."

Francine basked in the love of her grandparents and often enjoyed visits to their home.

When Francine was ten the family moved to Stillwater, Oklahoma, where Mercury Marine also had a big plant. Mark started working there, but left to go to work for the Sooner Generating Plant. Dee found a job at Oklahoma State University in the accounting department. They found a house on Arapaho Street in the northeast section of Stillwater.

Stillwater, Oklahoma is in the Bible belt of the nation. Few of the Methodists that knew Dee and Mark were aware they liked to relax in the evenings at the bars in Stillwater. They frequently spent time in Jakie Boy's lounge on Main Street, where some others from the softball team also liked to gather. They also liked to frequent the bars on the

"Strip", Washington street between Sixth street and University Avenue, where the college students hang out. Marie Sherwood was a friend of Dee's. She enjoyed Dee's ribald sense of humor and her "dirty" dancing at parties at her home. She felt it was harmless and that Dee's sense of humor was much like comedienne Rosanne Barr, astringent sounding, but with friendly humor beneath the pungent phrases.

Francine attended Will Rogers elementary school. At that time she was a slender, freckle-faced youngster, unsmiling and serious. Her teachers remember her as average to bright, painfully anxious to please. She rarely raised her hand, even when she knew the right answer. When she was called on she would blush a bright red and answer in a barely audible voice. Oral book reports were an agony for her, and some teachers recognized the young girl's extreme shyness and sympathized with her. At that time she wore her brilliant coppery hair long. She had braces on her teeth and she wore glasses to correct her myopia. Even at that early age, Francine had difficulty making friends. At times she would be overeager to please them and at other times she would withdraw.

In light of her family's attitudes, it is not surprising Francine had trouble making friends. There was the constant emphasis on secrecy and privacy "We don't tell other people where we go on weekends" and "We don't tell other people what we do at home."

When Dee wanted to berate or chastise Francine, she did so in no uncertain terms in language usually associated with the Navy. There was only one right way to do things, and that was Dee's way. Francine was told what to do, when to do it, and Dee brooked no argument.

This is not to say she didn't love Francine in her own way. Dee was proud of Francine's accomplishments and loved to brag to co-workers that she had the perfect, obedient child.

In the sixth grade, Francine attended the sixth grade learning center with all the other sixth graders from the city in one big facility. This was discontinued the next year, and Francine went to middle school for her seventh and eighth grades. Jana West remembers both Francine and Cindy from her time of working in the office at middle school. Neither girl was outstanding, but they appeared to her as normal, unremarkable girls.

Francine's parents were strict. She was not encouraged to bring friends home to spend the night. The main outside school activities she participated in at that time was girl scouting. Dee was an assistant leader. West of Stillwater near Lake Blackwell is Camp Sylvia Stapley where the Girl Scouts learn about nature, take hikes and camp out. Dee was always ready to volunteer for the Girl Scout camping activities. It is doubtful if Francine ever spent a night with the Girl Scouts without her mother being there. The women who were the other leaders appreciated Dee's and Mark's interest in Scouting. It is a rule that the adult leaders must stay awake all night during the camp-outs, so any parents willing to undertake this task are appreciated.

The security at Girl Scout camps today would be hard to understand, unless you were also aware of the murder of three little Girl Scouts at a Tulsa camp in the early 1980s.

One close friend of both Delores and Francine recalls that she, as well as Francine's mother, felt Francine was totally dependable. You could direct the girl to purchase something, hand her a twenty dollar bill and be assured she would bring back the correct change, with never a thought of spending some of the money on herself.

In middle school Francine asked to play in the band and her parents first rented and then purchased a tenor saxophone from Chenowith & Green Music store in Stillwater.

Band members, particularly in high school tend to form cliques of their own, apart from the regular clannish social activities of high school youths. Due to the rigors of early morning marching drills, required even when the weather is uncomfortably cold, band members tend to feel they are somewhat "tougher" than orchestra members, and look with scorn on the string instrument players.

Francine was never heard to complain. She was stoic about discomfort and the boys who played saxophone and sat next to her liked her and felt she was a good sport. When the band traveled to the Tri-State music festival in Enid, Francine laughed a lot. She rode the carnival rides with the group and seemed light hearted and happy. Mark and Dee volunteered and served as chaperones on one overnight band bus trip.

Pictures in the high school year book of Francine's sophomore year shows her wearing a T-shirt, faded jeans and sandals, which was almost a uniform for her. Her adolescent face seemed all eyes, nose, and teeth. Her hair, which should have been her best feature was pulled back, revealing large ears. There is a vulnerable look on her face as she peers into the camera lens.

Mark and Dee were gratified that the expense of the orthodontist had produced results. Francine asked for contact lenses, and her parents bought them for her. They were slightly tinted, which accented the emerald color of her eyes.

She took Spanish and French and belonged to both the Spanish and French Clubs. The language clubs met after school in the classrooms. Despite her evident longing to be accepted, she again chose to distance herself from the group. She would pick a desk at the farthest corner of the room. Francine seemed incapable of the inconsequential chatter and the banter that went on between her classmates. She was, for the most part, simply ignored.

Besides playing the tenor saxophone in the band, she was a Flag Girl in her sophomore year. Francine attended marching band exercises and flag twirling routines faithfully and did not complain, but appeared to thrive. In those activities she was not expected to say anything, indeed it is impossible to carry on a much of a conversation, so she was content.

The other flag girls recall that she would sometimes come to practice before school and it was apparent from both her attitude and her words, that she wished to be let alone "Don't touch me! Don't come near me! Just let me alone!" They had no idea what had upset Francine before she came to school, but evidently something had. The other girls on the team left her alone.

Her mother insisted that she take Accounting in high school, and she passed the course but was not at the top of her class. Francine also took Algebra I, II, and trigonometry and was invited to join Mu Alpha Theta, the mathematics honor society for students interested in higher math. Rosetta Silvers taught Francine in Algebra II. She remembers her primarily for the fact that Francine was an office aide and often helped school nurse Virginia Turvey giving eye and ear tests. This duty occasionally made Francine late for class. Mrs. Silvers would tell Francine to come to her after class, if she needed help or if she had missed part of the assignment. Francine was a quiet and unremarkable student, not at the top of the class, but not flunking, either.

At the start of her junior year in high school Francine surprised all the classmates who knew her by suddenly declaring that she would run for office in the Student Council elections. It was totally out of character for the girl who always chose the corner seat at the back of class, putting as much distance between herself and the rest of the class as possible. Classmates wondered what had prompted her to take this action, since when she was called upon to make her declaration speech in front of the entire student body, she barely finished one coherent sentence and sat down promptly. It was obvious she was terribly nervous and had not practiced before a mirror, indeed she had hardly practiced making the speech at all.

Her poorly drawn posters and banners were pathetically homemade looking. Either she naively thought it made no difference, or she lacked confidence to ask art students to help her in the campaign. Her slogan was: Make the Right Step with Stepp. She became the butt of ridicule and jokes. Some students who would have been willing to vote for her felt she did not deserve respect because it appeared she was making no real effort to conduct a serious campaign.

Francine was an office aide the next year, but she had already closed down her hopes of being accepted as one of the popular "in" crowd. It was after the debacle of the student council elections that Francine began to associate more and more with Cindy Wynn.

Francine had known Cindy Wynn and was friends with her, but it was only in the junior and senior years of high school that she began to spend time with Cindy exclusively.

They would sit at the back of the room, talking to each other before class. Cindy would talk loudly about the boys that wanted to marry her and how she couldn't decide which one to date on Saturday night. She would say, in theatrical tones, "I just don't know what to do, my boyfriend says he'll kill himself if I don't marry him, and I don't want to get married yet, I'm having too much fun!"

Some classmates thought it was rather pathetic. The two girls were not in the popular sororities or cliques and were trying to appear desirable. Several expressed regret to this writer that they had not been friendlier to Francine. Many of Francine's school classmates admitted while they were not cruel to Francine, they just ignored her. She was so quiet and self-effacing that it was easy to overlook her. This was not true of Cindy Wynn.

Cindy was an active member of the Hillcrest Baptist Youth Group. She went to church on Sunday evenings and was "saved" on more than one occasion. Members recall that on one bus trip home Cindy was sitting near the back of the bus. She let out a piercing, long drawn out scream and then slumped in her seat. The bus driver took her to the emergency room of the nearest hospital, where it was determined that she was suffering from a migraine headache. Some of the group felt at that time that she had "freaked out" while it is probably accurate to say that it is an example of Cindy's theatrical, histrionic personality.

Cindy was always the spokesperson for the duo. When a teacher would reprimand them for whispering or passing notes, Francine would duck her head, but Cindy would smile and often as not make some smart remark, hoping to amuse the class. Cindy was an indifferent student in high school, although she did belong to the Drama Club.

At parties during their high school years, Francine rarely did much other than sit in the corner, although she had started smoking cigarettes occasionally and drinking beer. Classmates swear that both girls used to take "Black Mollys" a speed pill available for one dollar each clandestinely. Cindy twice started altercations with different girls, screaming at them, and accusing them of trying to take her boyfriend away. Both young women remember being startled and shocked that Cindy appeared on the verge of physically assaulting them. Both women left the parties hurriedly, anxious to avoid any confrontation with Cindy. The boys involved seemed amused and as Cindy became more possessive in her attentions, annoyed with her. Cindy especially enjoyed stirring people up. A classmate recalls that during a first hour class she had with Cindy, Cindy would appear friendly. Then in second hour class, Cindy would relay false information to a mutual friend, who would be angered by the false information. There was no point in the rumor-mongering, other than it upset two people that Cindy evidently envied.

On another bus trip, Cindy loudly proclaimed to everyone sitting around her that her natural mother was a street hooker in Nashville, Tennessee and that she had forced Cindy into prostitution when she was only twelve years old. It was such an intolerable situation that she had come to live with her father in Stillwater. At least four people on the bus heard this story, but some felt it was simply another bid for attention and pity. If it was her aim to gain sympathy, it fell flat. Both Cindy and Francine apparently wanted the friendship and regard of others, but Cindy with her theatrics and Francine with her withdrawal failed to find the social group they desired.

David West taught both Francine and Cindy in Biological Science class. He seated the class alphabetically, and this put both Francine and Cindy near the rear of the class, but with rows of desks between. He observed the girls mouthing whispers to each other and passing notes. Often times it appeared to him that Cindy would be upset about something, and Francine would be comforting her, with an arm around her. West felt their behavior was more appropriate for sophomore students than for seniors in high school. He surmised that both girls were probably slightly emotionally delayed.

On one occasion the girls needed help starting a car. He recalls that it was one Cindy was driving. He obliged by bringing jumper cables, as they requested, but when he got to the car, found that the starter turned over readily. He turned to the girls and said, "What made you think you needed jumper cables?" They shrugged and replied that when a car wouldn't go, everyone sent for jumper cables.

West smilingly told them to check the fuel gauge more often. Then he took them to get a can of gas, and stayed with them until the car was started. Both Cindy and Francine were polite and thanked him effusively. He felt they were nice girls, evidently not too smart about the mechanics of automobiles, but nevertheless nice girls.

David Silvers taught both Francine and Cindy in Senior English class. He observed that Cindy was a bright, intelligent girl, but if there were any shortcuts, or any expedient way to do things she would. Occasionally she would try to shock or anger him by inappropriate comments in class. At those times, he would refuse to rise to her bait, and simply say, "That's inappropriate." A few times, when Cindy seemed determined to upset class routine, he would simply walk over and stand by her desk, letting his physical presence quell her into silence.

He remembers Francine as being very quiet and subdued and a model student. His son was one of the students interviewed by Fox Television for the TV program *A Current Affair*. His wife, Rosetta, recalls that she thought it a little unusual that Francine would ride the bus in her senior year of high school. It appeared to her that Francine must have strict parents, to insist that she rely on the school bus, instead of providing transportation. (Francine had a car, but was not allowed to drive it to school daily.) She remembers Mark Stepp attending the high school Open House. Fewer than one third of the students' parents attend the evening events, when parents can spend some time in each class room and talk with each student's teacher briefly. It is an indication that Mark Stepp cared for his daughter's success in school and is typical of his concern for his daughter.

It was Cindy's particular delight to shock and anger her parents by dating African-Americans. Francine followed her lead in this as in other things. In a stormy argument, Cindy moved out of her parents' house in her junior year of high school and from that time lived in several different homes in the area.

A studious young black man who dated Francine remembers her as a pleasant date, one who liked to play pool and listen when he talked. She was never a chatterbox, as Cindy was. They dated for about six weeks, and then Francine was "too busy" to go out. (She had met Fred Rank.)

Just two days before the murders, the motion picture *Colors* was showing in Stillwater. This movie about gangs in Los Angeles concerns racially motivated gang warfare and shows people being assaulted and killed in their homes by gang members. Cindy Wynn attended this movie with her black boyfriend, Randy Jackson.

It is doubtful if either Francine or Cindy had ever seen anyone die, or if either young woman had a realistic concept of death, up until the time of the murders. In an age when motion pictures and television prides itself on realism, young people may have seen many horror pictures of bodies being cut with chain saws, eyes gouged out, and so on. But while the youthful viewers can watch scenes that their elders would shudder over, it seems that few young people of today, have an understanding of the reality and finality of death.

When the actual deed was done, Cindy fled the scene in horror, shrieking, and Francine has experienced such repressed feelings and denial that she cannot talk about it. Although Oklahoma courts would not admit testimony drawn through hypnosis, and Francine would probably refuse to be hypnotized, it would be interesting if her memory could be unblocked, if only to aid scientists in better understanding the case and learning what motivated her.

Just as police are aware of the "bushy-haired stranger" that pops up frequently as the purported culprit, they are also aware that sometimes the killers have a need to "discover" the bodies of their victims.

Both young women express regret for the murders. Both young women will carry the weight of that moment with them forever.

After the murders, the house the Stepps lived in was locked up and stood vacant for a year. A group of nineteen and twenty-year-olds were arrested six months later for breaking and entering. The youths did not damage anything in the house, admitting they were simply curious to see where the murders had taken place.

The First National Bank held the mortgage on the house and it reverted back to the institution, since none of the Stepp relatives wanted it. The cars were sold through the bank at private auction, as were the household furnishings.

Despite the fact the Stepp home is not easy to find and parking was difficult, an unusually large crowd turned out for the Stepp household items auction. Many people were curious about the place where the murders had occurred and were eager to get a chance to see it. The bedroom door was kept locked, however, but the rest of the house was visible.

The Wynn's house, next door to the Stepps' home, located on the corner, was sold promptly after the couple left Stillwater in the fall, before Cindy Wynn received her final sentence. It is a nice neighborhood with friendly people nearby, people who regret the tragic events that transpired there.

A neighbor, Peggy Little, recalls the first time she met Cindy Wynn, riding down the street on her bicycle. She was favorably impressed by the openness and cheerfulness of the teenager. She still insists that the Cindy that lived near her was friendly, likable and kind to children, and she finds it hard to believe that Cindy had any part in planning or carrying out killings.

Why did the killings happen? Why did two young ladies from good homes with Sunday School backgrounds plan and carry out the murders? There is the element of tragically mismatched personalities. Francine learned early on in life that to reveal her distress by crying or complaining only subjected her to more discipline. She became even more introverted and withdrawn than she naturally was.

Mark and Delores Stepp were not evil people. They truly loved their daughter and provided for her, believing they were doing a good job as parents. It was in the nature of their personalities to be self-centered, opinionated and given to superficial judgments. Had they looked below the surface of the apparently docile young daughter, they would have seen a raging cauldron of conflicts including a great deal of anger directed at them.

No one likes to believe the worst about the people closest to them. Delores and Mark closed their eyes to clues that would have told them their daughter needed help. Had the family gone for counseling, had they received professional help things might have turned out differently.

Afterword

The names of Fred Rank, John Biggsley, Jeff Adams and Randy Jackson are not the real names of the actual persons involved. Their names have been changed to protect their privacy.

Francine Marie Stepp

Cindy Sue Wynn

Delores, Mark and Francine Stepp

Exterior of Stepp home.

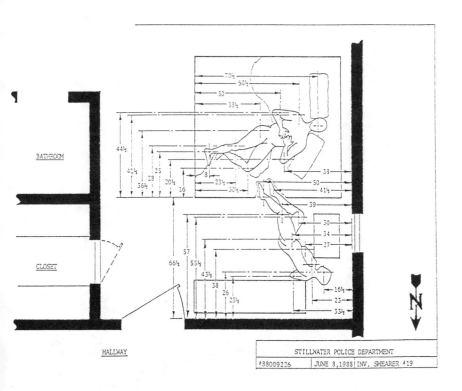

STILLWATER POLICE DEPARTMENT

#38009226 | JUNE 3,1938 | INV. SHEARER #19

BATHROOM

CLOSET

HALLWAY

Position of bodies when found in bedroom.

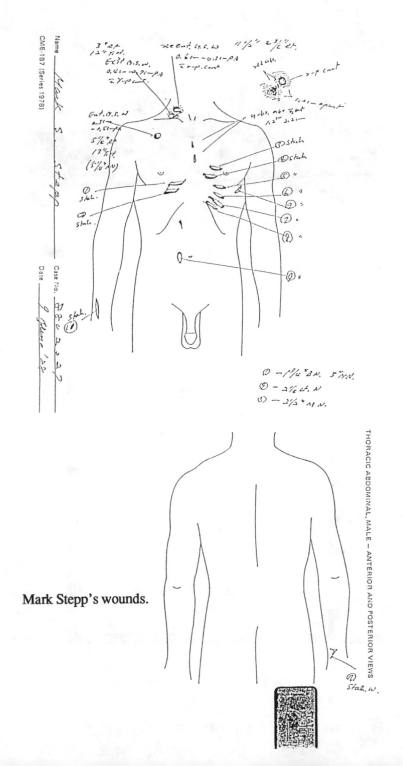

Mark Stepp's wounds.

FULL BODY, FEMALE — ANTERIOR AND POSTERIOR VIEWS

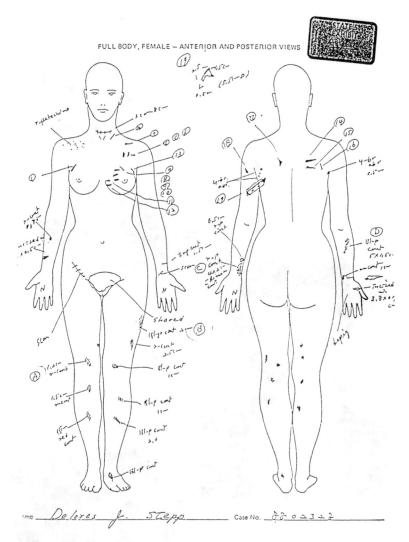

Delores Stepp's wounds.

Cpl Dennis McGrath

Lt. Ron Thrasher

District Attorney
Paul Anderson

Stillwater Police Headquarters

Payne County courthouse and jail (in basement).

Mabel Bassett Correctional Center

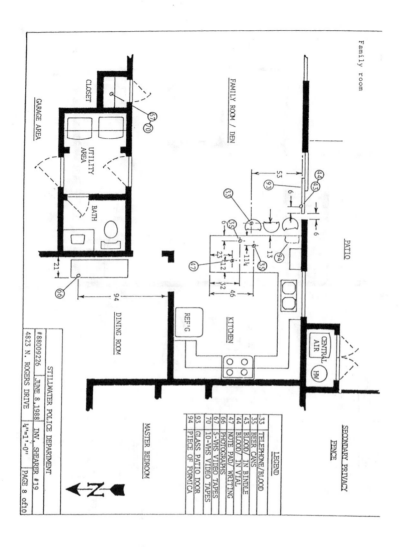

Family room

FAMILY ROOM / DEN

CLOSET

GARAGE AREA

UTILITY AREA

BATH

PATIO

SECONDARY PRIVACY FENCE

CENTRAL AIR
HW

KITCHEN

REF'G

DINING ROOM

MASTER BEDROOM

LEGEND
33	TELEPHONE/BLOOD
35	BEER CANS
43	BLOOD/ IN BINDLE
44	BLOOD/ IN VIAL
47	NOTE PAD/ WRITING
66	PHOTOGRAPHS
67	S-VHS VIDEO TAPES
70	10-VHS VIDEO TAPES
93	GLASS PATIO DOOR
94	PIECE OF FORMICA

STILLWATER POLICE DEPARTMENT
#88009226 | JUNE 8,1988 | INV. SHEARER #19
4823 N. ROGERS DRIVE | ¼"=1'-0" | PAGE 8 of 10

N

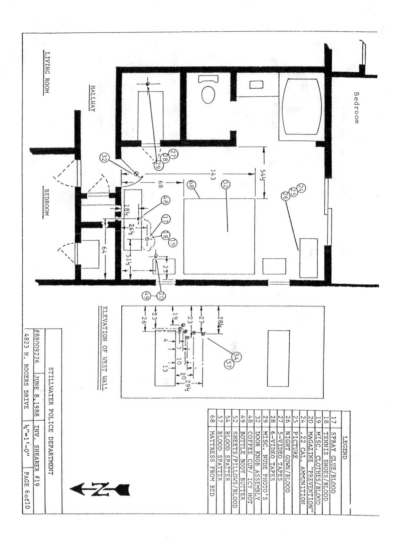

LIVING ROOM

HALLWAY

BEDROOM

Bedroom

ELEVATION OF WEST WALL

N

STILLWATER POLICE DEPARTMENT
#88009226 | JUNE 8,1988 | INV. SHEARER #19
4823 N. ROGERS DRIVE | ¼"=1'-0" | PAGE 6of10

	LEGEND
17	SPRAY GLUE/BLOOD
18	TENNIS SHOES/BLOOD
19	MISC. CLOTHES/BLOOD
20	MAGAZINE "PREVENTION"
24	.22 CAL. AMMUNITION
25	PICTURE
26	NIGHT GOWN/BLOOD
27	5-VIDEO TAPES
28	6-VIDEO TAPES
29	MISC. NUDE PHOTO'S
32	DOOR KNOB ASSEMBLY
48	COFFEE CUP/ ICY HOT
49	BOTTLE BODY BUTTER
52	SHEETS/PILLOWS/BLOOD
54	BLOOD SPATTER
57	BLOOD SPATTER
68	MATTRESS FROM BED

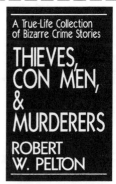